The Best Little Book of

Preserves & Pickles

The Best Little Book of

Preserves & Pickles

EASY jams & jellies, chutneys & condiments, sauces, spreads & syrups

Red Rock Press   New York, NY

Judith Choate

Design by Susan Smilanic, Studio 21 Design & Advertising

Index by Sayre Van Young

Choate, Judith.
 The best little book of preserves & pickles : easy jams & jellies,
chutneys & condiments, sauces, spreads & syrup / by Judith Choate.
     p. cm.
 Includes index.
 ISBN 978-1-933176-37-6
 1. Condiments. 2. Pickled foods. I. Title.
 TX819.A1C496 2011
 641.4'62--dc22

                                                    2010048669

2/2012.
3853 7525

For Lynn, the best friend a girl could have

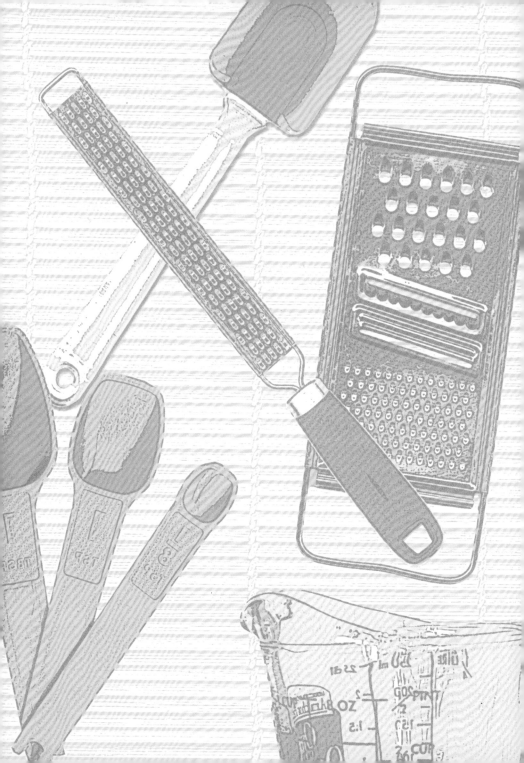

Table of Contents

INTRODUCTION

No matter how superb or unusual the commercial product, it will never equal the *ultimate* preserves made in your own kitchen.

This book is for the experienced cook who wants to produce small amounts of the very best preserves. Sweet or savory, spread, sauce or condiment, these are recipes to give your own menus that extra gusto and to provide the perfect on-hand gift for fellow food lovers. Although canning often carries with it no small measure of fear (even in the mind of the most accomplished cook!), it is really quite a simple kitchen task that, once tried, will often become a favorite pastime since the results are so rewarding.

The surge of interest in foods American, the proliferation of restaurants featuring American cuisine and the Americanization of international recipes have led us back to the discovery of our native cuisine.

Our regenerated preference for fruits and vegetables grown in our own gardens or nearby — locavore, if you will — and so requiring little time and fuel to reach our kitchen also inspires us to preserve seasonal bounty.

Our forefathers ate and preserved far more foods than most contemporary Americans will ever taste. Many foods that we now consider special were frequently on the average person's plate in the early 20th century: game, wild greens, "free range" chicken, unadulterated meats, native herbs and fruits. Items for which we will now pay extra were once just plain food. It is interesting to note that gourmet preserving is not new, just rediscovered.

The history of "putting foods by" has been greatly enhanced by American ingenuity. From the early colonists' preservation of new and different native foodstuffs for times of scarcity to the invention of freeze-dried meals in the 20th century, Americans have constantly created inventive ways to store foods. However, it was the advent of the 19th-century Shaker communities that most profoundly affected American preserving.

The Shakers' arrival in America, in 1774, marked a time of change and freedom, a time for new thought and creation. Then, when the Revolution freed the colonies from England, its newly-minted citizens strove to establish a truly American life. Having brought traditional preserving methods with them from the Old Country, Americans began to expand their preserving skills using regional American produce. Martha Washington, as First Lady, became an advocate of American cooking, and culinary invention flourished.

By the mid-1860s, the Shaker community had grown from seven members to several communities with thousands of members in many states. Each community not only was self-sufficient but grew and made enough to sell to the outside world. Shaker kitchens were models of efficiency and cleanliness and were the earliest example of mass production. The canning kitchens were equipped (and still are, in both museum and contemporary living settlements) with huge stoves, great copper canning kettles and pristine spaces in cupboards and on long trestle tables to facilitate the production of preserved foods. Filled with advanced conveniences and inventions, the Shaker canning kitchen created a demand in the general public for products carrying the Shaker label. The quality, integrity and care that characterized these products established, for the American housewife, a high standard to duplicate in her own kitchen.

In fact, in areas where Shaker communities flourished it was not at all unusual for an outside family to take its own produce to be preserved by the Shaker sisters. Their recipes used the best they could grow, were seasoned with imagination and were stored in the most beautifully crafted containers they could create. Not only did they cook, they did so with inventiveness, skill and with the knowledge that food was one of God's rewards. This is the heritage that is the basis for the current interest in our native cuisine, of which preserving the best foodstuffs a cook has at hand is an integral part.

The wide availability of a variety of fresh fruits, vegetables and herbs has now made it possible to prepare canned goods all year long. However, it is always preferable to use local products during their individual growing seasons. And, of course, locally and organically grown products offer the cook the additional assurance of quality. January's picture-perfect, flavorless tomato, the stored apple of March and the year-round frozen strawberry all have a fraction of the taste, smell and texture of their garden-fresh counterparts. When feasible, I recommend that you do your preserving seasonally. When this is not possible, purchase the best available from a supermarket, greengrocer or local wholesaler. You can also experiment with the exotic produce now imported from around the world for American consumption. The end result will be well worth the extra time, effort and money you put into selecting quality ingredients for your gourmet preserves.

What are gourmet preserves? Unique combinations, careful flavoring, color and pure, clean taste are the most important components of what should be a welcome addition to any menu and should turn a mundane meal into an extraordinary dining experience. They should be produced from the finest quality ingredients, organically and locally grown if at all possible. No grape jelly or ordinary dill pickles here!

Sophisticated preserves have evolved from our American culinary heritage. They combine the best of the old with the convenience and availability of the new. It is the legacy of our forefathers (and mothers), the integrity and ingenuity of the Shakers and the cook's flare for experimentation and discriminating taste that combine to produce gourmet preserves. Every wonderful food that we know as American can be brought to the table from a bag, a carton, a jar, a can or a crock. Just let this book be your guide.

14

CHAPTER 1

THE RIGHT INGREDIENTS

Three Little Words: Fresh, Fresh, Fresh

Looking through my grandmother's canning notes, I found this cardinal rule: "One hour from garden to can." This is generally impossible today and, with modern refrigeration and storage, no longer really necessary. However, fresh is best!

All fruits and vegetables should be firm, free of blemishes and as recently picked as possible. Fruits should be well ripened and vegetables crisp. The question about whether organically-grown is better can only be answered by the quality of the produce before your eyes. Organically-grown does not invariably guarantee excellent quality. Only you can judge as you select. In addition, organic produce that travels thousands of miles has enormous impact on the environment that offsets its original intent. Unless otherwise specified, all ingredients in a given recipe should be of consistent high quality and ripeness.

If you garden, or have a farmer's market or orchard nearby, you can be assured of freshness. I generally do most of my canning and preserving in season with produce from my garden or from local farmers markets (both in the city and in the country) or from country farm stands. In these instances, organically grown products are to be recommended. If you must rely on your supermarket produce manager or neighborhood greengrocer, make friends, give bribes and pay extra to get the best obtainable. It is smart, both for economy and taste, to do as much preserving as you can during your area's growing season. The finished product is only enhanced by the perfection of the ingredients.

As new and unusual produce (and other food products) are imported from around the world, try to incorporate them into your preserving. I am constantly amazed at the availability of fresh herbs, tropical produce and exotic vegetables, and I have experimented with all of them. If you see an untried fruit or vegetable, buy a small amount for tasting and comparing. Once you have identified its properties, adapt it to your usual recipes. For instance, all berries are just about interchangeable. And kiwi can be used in place of any soft, juicy fruit. Don't be afraid to experiment. If you do so in small batches, you can generally enjoy a new taste treat or salvage what could have been a disaster.

All of the products used in preserving — seasonings, herbs, dried fruits or vegetables, chocolate and so forth — should be of the highest quality. Imported or most expensive is not necessarily the best, so do some research before buying. Each recipe will give a recommended type or style, but you might also want to experiment with what is available to you.

Clean all ingredients thoroughly. Leafy vegetables, berries and herbs should be inspected for sand or grit. A spray wash will assist in removing it. Root vegetables should be scrubbed.

Dry thoroughly. Fragile foods such as berries should be drained dry on towels or paper.

Peaches, nectarines, apricots and tomatoes are easily peeled by marking one end with a gentle "X" and then immersing, for about 30 seconds, in a pot of boiling water to loosen the skin. Quickly remove from the boiling water and dip into cold water. The skin will generally slip off ripe fruit and, with a bit of assistance with a paring knife, off not-so-ripe fruit.

Berries are stemmed and are usually left whole. All other fruits and vegetables should be stemmed, peeled or skinned, seeded and cut as directed in a specific recipe.

If a recipe calls for cooked fruits or vegetables, add the least amount of water you can to prevent sticking. I generally add no water for soft fruits and vegetables and no more than one cup per quart for raw, hard fruits or vegetables. Cover and simmer over very low heat until the fruit or vegetable is just cooked through. Do not overcook if it is being used in a recipe that requires further cooking.

All other ingredients should be fresh and measured out before proceeding with the recipe. This will make the processing much simpler as well as ensure that you have everything you need on hand before continuing with the final preparation.

Preserving Without Sugar

In preserving, sugar is used not only to sweeten but to retain flavor, texture and color as well as to aid in the prevention of spoilage during long-term storage. It does not, alone, prevent spoilage. Since there are now so many cooks who must address health issues in the kitchen, I offer just a few hints to preserve with sweeteners other than the traditional cane or beet sugar.

Alternative Sugars

Traditional sugar may be replaced, wholly or in part, with honey, corn syrup, maple syrup or fruit juice. Honey, corn syrup and maple syrup all affect both the color and flavor of the finished product. Honey or corn syrup can replace half of the sugar while maple syrup can only be used to replace one-quarter. The color of dark corn syrup, dark honey, molasses or other dark or strong-flavored syrups will radically change the color and flavor of the finished product. In all instances, when using a commercial pectin, you must follow the manufacturer's directions for sugar replacement. If using no commercial pectin, the thickening process will generally require substantially more cooking time.

Sugar Replacements

Non-nutritive sweeteners required for those with specific health issues, such as diabetes, have had their own issues. Some impart a metallic taste or aftertaste. Others work well.

In recent years, with the development of more refined sugar replacements, much of the unpleasantness associated with non-nutritive sugar replacements has diminished. I have had luck using Splenda® Granular No Calorie Sweetener and agave syrup, although with both I have found a flatness in the sweetness of the finished product. With Splenda® Granular No Calorie Sweetener it is necessary to use pectin products made specifically for canning and preserving using sugar replacements, such as

Mrs. Wage's ™ Lite Home Jell® Fruit Pectin, Ball® No-Sugar Needed Pectin, Pomona's Universal Pectin or Sure-Jell® for Less or No Sugar-Needed Recipes. Each type will come with directions.

When using Splenda® Granular No Calorie Sweetener in any of the recipes in this book, you must use under-ripe fruit or vegetables as they will contain the necessary amount of natural pectin. This is because as fruits or vegetables naturally ripen, the natural pectin they contain decreases. Overly ripe fruit or vegetables will usually result in an end result that has either a soft set or no set at all.

Agave syrup, a natural product made from the agave plant, is 40% sweeter than sugar, has a very low-glycemic index (important to diabetics) and leaves no unpleasant aftertaste. It is readily soluble in liquid and is versatile in canning and preserving.

If, for a medical reason, you're planning to use any sugar substitute, it's a good idea to check with your physician or medical advisor.

It is very important to note that when using Splenda® Granular No Calorie Sweetener or other non-nutritive sugar replacements, it is essential that proper canning and preserving techniques be followed. Since non-nutritive sweeteners do not have the same preservative qualities as natural sugar, they do not aid in the prevention of spoilage. It is absolutely necessary that you follow both recommended preserving measures as well as the manufacturer's direction given for the specific pectin used.

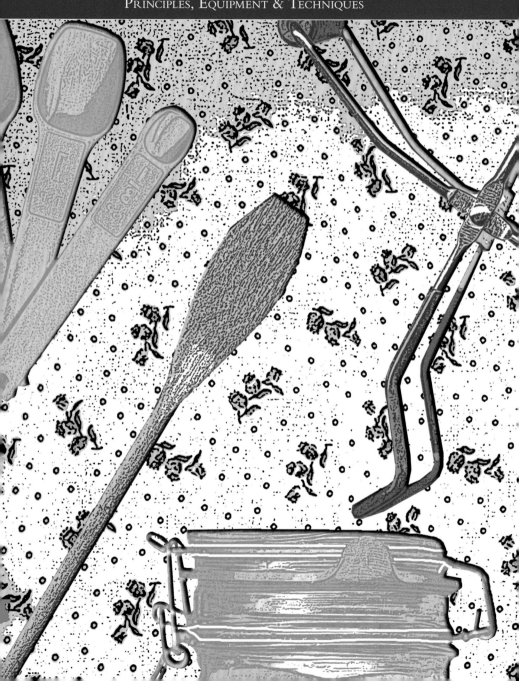

First Principles

- Always plan in advance. Preserving is not a spur-of-the-moment inspiration.
- Familiarize yourself with the processes you will be using. Like general cooking, preserving is much easier when you don't have to remember the basics while involved in the step-by-step routine.
- Your equipment must be clean, free of cracks, chips or rust. Spoilage is frequently caused by the use of unclean or damaged equipment.
- Keep your work area uncluttered and free of unnecessary utensils or jars.
- Use the exact ingredients as directed in each recipe.
- Make sure you have sufficient containers with lids that fit. (I generally sterilize a couple of extra jars and lids, just in case I end up with more to can than the recipe states.)
- Prepare only the exact amount of fruit or vegetables required. Everything in each batch should be of the same ripeness and quality.
- Measure out the ingredients before you begin. This will ensure against the loss of a batch of preserves when an essential ingredient is, at the last and most inopportune moment, missing.
- When using the water bath method, be certain you are familiar with its cooking processes.
- Keep all jars and lids in their hot sterilizing baths until ready for use. Remove one jar at a time.

All canning jars must be hot when being filled with hot foods
or liquids.

- Fill and seal one container at a time.
- No matter what processing method is used, all lids, rims and
edges must be clean and free of food before sealing.
- Always cool filled jars before placing in the freezer or on a very
cold surface.
- Label everything you preserve with its name, date and shelf life.
- And, above all, don't rush! There are NO safe shortcuts to be
taken when making gourmet preserves.

The Right Equipment

Most equipment required for gourmet preserving will be
found on your kitchen shelves, as you will need nothing out of the
ordinary. Since we are dealing with quality rather than quantity,
you will not even need the huge canning kettles required for the
basic preserving of the past.

More than any other modern convenience, the food processor
has eliminated much of the drudgery of kitchen chores. As an aid
in preserving, it zests, chops, blends and peels with the least waste
and mess. As a time saver, it is even better!

All of your equipment must be very clean and free of rust,
chips or scratches.

You Will Want to Have on Hand

- Food processor (a blender, food grater or food mill can also be used)
- Heavy kettle for cooking jams, jellies, relishes, etcetera
- Large pot (with lid) for use as a boiling water bath or water bath canner
- Measuring cups and spoons
- Wooden spoons
- Large metal spoon
- Funnel
- Ladle with pouring spout
- Spatula
- Jar lifter or tongs
- Strainer (a colander with cheesecloth or a sieve can also be used)
- Clean cloths for wiping jars

Extras (not necessary but nice to have)

- Kitchen scale
- Wire racks for cooling
- Jelly bag
- Prepared labels

Canning Jars

You can, in most areas, purchase home canning jars at a grocery, hardware or variety store. Fancy canning jars are frequently featured in gourmet food and cookware catalogs.

If you have any difficulty locating standard canning jars locally, there are many, many sources available through the internet (see Sources, page 185).

• The can or freeze jar may be used for either home canning or freezing. This jar will require the standard two-part metal cover, which consists of a flat rubber-edged sealing lid and a screw cap.
• The lightening jar is used for canning outside the United States. It has a glass domelike lid that seals with a rubber ring. The lid is held tight by a wire clamp. The U.S. Department of Agriculture does not consider this jar a safe choice.

A jar must be freshly sterilized and free of soap or odors. All rubber sealing lids or rings should be unused and sterile.

Canners

There are two types of home-preserving canners: water bath and steam pressure. In this book, all the recipes requiring canning will call for a water bath simply because none of the products require the heat and pressure gained from steam pressure canning

A water bath canner is a deep kettle with a wire basket insert that holds about eight jars. The kettle will hold enough water to cover the jars without boiling over. It is used to preserve foods high in acids that do not require the high pressure of a steam pressure canner.

If you decide you are going to do extensive home canning, however, you may want to purchase a steam pressure canner, available at most kitchenware shops. A large pressure cooker holds about 22 quarts and has a tight-fitting lid and a steam valve. This kettle is used to process foods under pressure at high temperatures. It is the only home method that will destroy the bacteria that causes botulism and other severe types of spoilage in low-acid foods, such as meat, poultry and seafood as well as any vegetable mixture not containing vinegar, citrus juice or sugar.

Both types of canners require special attention to the manufacturer's instructions.

Preparing Containers

All preserving containers must be clean, free of any damage and appealing to look at.

Containers and lids (other than sealed plastic bags) must be washed in hot, soapy water and well rinsed in hot water before use.

When using a boiling water bath, you must use a container that can withstand the period of time required in boiling water. Commercial canning jars are best suited for this.

To sterilize jars: In a large pot, cover jars and lids with hot water. Bring to a rapid boil and boil for 10 minutes. Remove from the heat. Keep jars in water until ready to use. If water cools down, or for some reason you get interrupted, place pot back over the heat and bring to a boil again.

If recipe calls for a clean, hot container, wash and rinse as directed above. Cover jars and lids with boiling water. Keep them in hot water until ready to use.

Some home dishwashers are hot enough to use for the sterilization of jars. By all means, use one if you can. However, the jars still must be hot and sterile when filled.

METHODS OF PRESERVING

Preserving is, quite simply, a method of holding foods, sealed and free of contamination, for future eating and is, as such, an ancient ritual. I would guess that as soon as man discovered food he discovered a way to "put it by."

To prevent starvation, early man is presumed to have dried those foods available to him in times of plenty. Fire and salt expanded his preserving repertoire and freezing was improvised as a measure to keep foods longer. Until the 1800s, these were the only preserving methods available.

Canning, the results of which line our supermarket shelves, was an early 19th-century American invention. However, tin cans did not come into widespread use until after 1885, when a machine that stamped them out was patented. This offered a surefire method of preserving all manner of foodstuffs and took canning out of the home and into commerce.

Refrigeration greatly increased the life of all foods, both in the home and in the marketplace. The advent of the iceman brought the storage of perishable goods into the kitchen. The root cellar and cold storage were replaced with the icebox. Mechanical refrigeration further revolutionized food storage and greatly expanded year-round availability of produce from around the world. By the end of World War II, almost every kitchen had an electric refrigerator that offered some freezing capacity.

Quick freezing is, of course, the latest technique for the home preservation of food. It is less time-consuming than the other, older methods and generally the one that most nearly reproduces the flavor of the original.

No matter which method is used, there is no snappy way to produce gourmet preserves. Recipes must be followed and each preserving method learned. If you don't have time to do it, don't start. (The only exception to this rule is: You may prepare the raw produce and have all ingredients ready up to 24 hours prior to actual processing.)

All of the early methods remain today, many with little change. To preserve foods you may dehydrate, smoke, salt, cool, freeze or can. With gourmet preserves, however, we will deal only with the canning, freezing or refrigeration of fruits, vegetables (in many guises) and sauces. Each recipe will give a recommended method that must be followed. Again, do not take shortcuts!

Water Bath

This is used for jams, jellies, conserves, marmalades, butters, spiced fruit, chutneys, most cooked sauces, some cooked relishes, condiments, whole fruit and acidic vegetables. It requires that the food be cooked to boiling, in either a sugar or a vinegar base that assists in preservation, and immediately poured into hot, sterilized jars that are sealed with sterilized, rubber-edged lids and screw caps.

Filled clean, hot jars are processed on a rack in a deep pot (with lid) covered with boiling water for a stated period of time. Most products preserved in a water bath canner have a one-year shelf life.

General directions for water bath canning: In a pot made specifically for canning or a cooking pot large enough to hold the number of jars you are going to process completely submerged in water, bring water to a near boil. Place a rack on the bottom of the pot.

Fill, clean, hot jars with prepared food to be preserved, leaving one-half-inch headspace in each filled jar (unless otherwise specified). Remove air bubbles from jars by pushing around edge of jar with a rubber spatula. Wipe sealing edges clean with a dry cloth. Place lid and cap on each jar and twist closed. Do not seal tightly.

Place jars on rack at the bottom of the pot, allowing free circulation of the boiling water around and under each jar. The water must be at least three inches above tops of jars (add water if necessary). Bring to a boil as quickly as possible. When water is at a vigorous boil, begin counting off the processing time necessary for the individual recipe.

When processing time is reached, using tongs, remove jars from boiling water bath. Complete the seal by tightening screw cap. Invert jars. (This will test for leaks.)

After about 10 minutes, set jars upright. Place about two inches apart on wire racks or newspaper, out of drafts, to cool.

Label.

Store in a cool, dry place.

Refrigeration

Refrigeration is a method generally used for foods that will be consumed quickly, either cooked or raw. There will be a few recipes that, due to the inclusion of either alcohol or vinegar-based liquid, will have a long refrigeration life. However, unless otherwise specified, most refrigerated preserves will have a very short shelf life.

General directions for refrigerated gourmet preserves: Fill clean, hot containers with prepared food. Wipe sealing edges with a clean, dry cloth. Seal with an airtight cover.

If necessary, cool to room temperature.

Label.

Refrigerate. To speed cooling, place in coldest part of re-frigerator for about three hours, with air space of at least one inch on all sides. Store in the refrigerator for no more than the suggested maximum storage period given in each recipe.

Freezing

This method is used for anything except those foods (such as pickles) in which the freezing and thawing process will break down the texture, resulting in an unappealing product. Its success depends more than any other preserving method on the quality of the fresh fruit or vegetable. Either one must be extremely fresh. Frozen cooked foods have a shelf life of approximately 8 to 12 months.

General directions for frozen preserves: Fill sterilized containers with fresh cold foods. Remove as much air as possible from the container by turning a spatula around the edges and tamping down. Leave enough headspace for food to expand during the freezing process. Wipe sealing edges with a clean, dry cloth. Seal with an absolutely airtight lid.

Label with date of freezing and maximum date for use.

Freeze immediately. It is essential that your freezer be at least zero degrees Fahrenheit or below while the freezing process is taking place. A stable, freezing temperature will ensure high quality. It is suggested that you do not overload your freezer when freezing gourmet preserves. Most manufacturers recommend that you add no more than two pounds per cubic foot of freezer space for quick freezing.

Each method has its use. In some recipes a choice will be given, in others only one method is suggested. In the latter case, please follow the suggestion for the best possible results. I reiterate: There are NO shortcuts.

Note that if you decide to use refrigeration or freezing as your preserving method, you need not first process in a water bath (or steam canner). But your prepared food may not last as long as you think! Please pay attention to shelf life given for each preserving and storing method.

SEALING PRESERVED FOODS

Water Bath Sealing

Foods preserved by the water bath method will make their own vacuum seal during processing. Those foods preserved by refrigeration or freezing are not usually vacuum-sealed, but they must be stored in absolutely airtight, lidded containers or in tightly sealed plastic bags.

Labeling & Storing

If you are going to do a lot of preserving, it is nice to have the extra touch of a personalized label. You can purchase decorated labels from many card shops, catalogues, specialty food shops or through the internet (see Sources, page 185). Or, if you buy standard canning jars, labels are usually included in the carton.

If computer savvy, you can print your own labels. It's also possible to order from a local printer labels with a line on which to handwrite the name of your preserve, as well as spots for the date preserved, shelf life and your name. You might have fun working with a printer to pick an appropriate style.

If you want to keep labeling simple, just purchase sheets of gummed labels or roll labels from a stationery store and hand-write or type the necessary information on each one.

No matter how you choose to do it, you must label! List the date, shelf life and contents on each jar or container. Uniform labeling, about two inches from the bottom of the container, will make your stacked jars look very attractive.

All recipes in this book have specific storing directions. Most will be vacuum-sealed in a water bath, some will require refrigeration, while a few might be suitable for freezing. In each case, the individual recipe will make note of these possibilities. In these instances, follow normal refrigeration and freezer precautions.

For best results, store all canned foods in a cool, dark place for no longer than one year. Foods may be stored longer, but occasionally the color and the taste will begin to fade.

Presentation

You don't have to shout, "I made it myself!" if you take care to present your homemade preserves with the same attention you gave to making them.

If you label each container with an attractive sticker, you will not need much more. However, canning jars seem to lend themselves to caps cut from pretty fabric prints. Cut a circle of fabric about one inch larger in diameter than the lid (pinking shears give you an even more attractive edge). Tie the circle around the cap with ribbon, colored cord or cotton string. Be sure to choose colors that compliment the color of the contents.

If you want to use your homemade products as gifts, you might wish to enhance one either with another homemade food, such as scones with Rhubarb Ginger Jam. Or you might give Salsa Inferno with a piece of purchased, hand-thrown Mexican pottery.

Using your own homemade preserves can only add to your gourmet table. So many cooks make everything from scratch and then use purchased jams, sauces or other condiments. A simple grilled hamburger (and not one grilled over a mesquite fire) becomes a gourmand's treat when served with homemade

Blueberry Catsup or Red Pepper Mustard. And you certainly wouldn't serve a commercial syrup over homemade ice cream.

Presentation is in the eye of both the maker and beholder. Use your culinary skill to its best advantage. Package your goods in beautiful containers and use them to intensify the fine taste of your gourmet meals.

CHAPTER 3

JELLIES, JAMS & PRESERVES

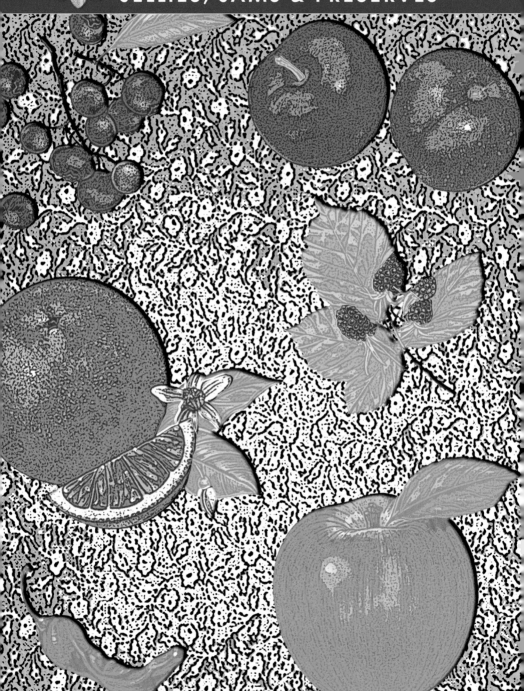

Jellies, jams and preserves differ only in texture, and although different, they all must gel. Each has the same four basic components: fruit for flavor; sugar for preserving, sweetness and consistency; acid for thickening; pectin for gelling. Jelly will be a clear, soft, solid mass while jams and preserves are full-fruited and can be either runny or firm depending on your preference.

The fruit in each should be of the highest quality and of uniform ripeness. (An exception; if you are not using commercial pectin, the ratio of ripe to under-ripe fruit should be four to one.) Discard fruit that shows signs of bruising or spoilage. Remove stems. For jams and preserves: core, seed and peel (unless using seeds and peels for pectin). For jelly: cook entire fruit for its juice. Prepare as directed in individual recipes.

Adding Acid

Fresh lemon juice, cider or apple vinegars are the usual added acids. Tart or under-ripe apples, crab apples, cranberries, tart grapes, blackberries and plums do not require additional acid for thickening, but lemon or grapefruit juice is frequently added to enhance the flavor.

Considering Pectin

Most of the recipes I use call for commercial pectin. There are some pectins on the market that require about one third less sugar than the usual commercial pectins require, and will result in a fresh-tasting jam, jelly or preserve. Unless otherwise stated in a recipe, follow the directions on the brand of pectin you use.

If you choose to cook without commercial pectin, you must adjust the ratio of sugar to fruit. Peels and cores contain much of the natural pectin in fruits, so retain them when possible. Tart apples are very high in natural pectin; therefore their juice may be used to supplement pectin in other fruits.

Jellies are made from the juice of cooked fruits or vegetables, extracted by dripping the fruit through a cloth jelly bag. Patience is required to make a sparkling clear jelly, as you may not squeeze or cajole juice through the bag or your jelly will be cloudy.

If you are not using commercial pectin, the juice is combined with sugar in the ratio of two-thirds cup sugar to one cup juice.

To extract juice from fruit and vegetables: Wash and dry the fruit or vegetable. Cut away all damaged parts. Cut fruit or vegetable into chunks. Do not peel or core (the exception to this is pineapple, which should be peeled). Place fruit or vegetable in heavy kettle. Add one cup water for each quart of hard fruit (such as apples or cranberries). Soft fruits and berries should be gently crushed to get the juice flowing. (If additional liquid is necessary, try not to add more than one cup of water to help prevent scorching.) Bring to a boil over high heat. Lower the heat to medium, stirring frequently. Hard fruit or vegetables will need approximately 30 minutes to extract juice, soft fruit and berries about 10 minutes. Do not overcook, as this will decrease the flavor and pectin. Remove from the heat. Pour food and juices into a wet jelly bag (or a colander lined with lightweight cotton or a double piece of cheesecloth) placed over a bowl or pot large enough to hold the dripping juice. Let drip for about 12 hours for clear juice. Do not squeeze bag. Use clear juice only. Discard all residue in the jelly bag.

Jams are made of crushed fruit. The fruit is combined with sugar in the proportion of one-half to two-thirds cup sugar to one cup fruit, if you are not using commercial pectin.

Preserves are made from berries, cherries, sliced or quartered fruit, cut-up vegetables or melon rinds. When not using commercial pectin, from three-quarters to one cup sugar to one cup fruit is used. Preserved fruits should retain their shape and be plump, clear and tender.

My younger son calls me the expert at runny jelly, jam and preserves. I say if it's runny, it has more uses. A great excuse to cover failure but, in truth, it's an example of turning failure to your advantage. Runny jams or preserves make great dessert toppings, cake fillings and savory-sauce bases and can be used on toast if you hold the slice flat. Runny jelly is perfect for glazes and dessert toppings and, if you spread it on lightly, it won't even run off the edge of your bread.

JELLIES

Jalapeño Jelly • Port Wine Jelly • Horseradish Jelly • Cassis Jelly • Herb or Mint Jellies • Orange Sauterne Jelly • Ginger Apple Jelly • Champagne Jelly • Framboise Jelly

JAMS

Spiced Tomato Jam • Maryella Mixon's Winter Blueberry Jam • Blackberry Brandy Jam • Fresh Fig Jam • Basil Jam •

Pennsylvania Peach Jam • Strawberry Grand–Marnier Jam •
Annie McDonagh's Rhubarb Ginger Jam • Sambuca Romana Jam •
Bar–le–Duc Jam

PRESERVES

Mom's Special Strawberry Preserves • Kumquat Grand–Marnier
Preserves • Shaker Green Tomato Preserves • Pure Raspberry
Preserves • Black Forest Preserves • Papaya Lime Preserves •
Ginger Pear Preserves

JALAPEÑO JELLY

QUANTITY	FOUR ½-PINT JARS
METHOD & SHELF LIFE	WATER BATH – 1 YEAR REFRIGERATION – 6 WEEKS

You can almost guarantee that Jalapeño Jelly will be served at some point during a visit to the American South. I'm not sure why, but this piquant, multipurpose jelly is a Southern favorite. It is generally used as an hors d'oeuvre with cream cheese on water biscuits. You can also use it as a glaze for meats, game and poultry or as an accompaniment to meats or game.

2 medium green bell peppers, preferably organic,
   seeded and sliced
¾ cup chopped jalapeño (or serrano) chilies,
   preferably organic
1½ cups distilled white vinegar
6½ cups sugar
1 6-ounce bottle liquid pectin
1 tablespoon dried red pepper flakes
Green food coloring (optional)

Combine the bell peppers and jalapeños in bowl of food processor fitted with the metal blade. Add the vinegar and, using quick on-and-off turns, process until finely ground. Scrape the pepper mixture into a heavy saucepan. Stir in sugar. Cook over high heat, stirring constantly, until liquid comes to a full, rolling boil. Boil for 10 minutes.

Remove from the heat. Stir in liquid pectin, red pepper flakes and 2 to 3 drops food coloring, if desired. Immediately pour into hot, sterilized jar. Cap and process for 10 minutes in a boiling water bath as directed on pages 30-32.

PORT WINE JELLY

QUANTITY	FOUR ½-PINT JARS
METHOD & SHELF LIFE	WATER BATH − 1 YEAR REFRIGERATION − 6 WEEKS

Probably derived from the old English port wine dessert gelatin, Port Wine Jelly is a tasty addition to your gourmet preserves. It can be made from other rich red wines, and apple juice may be substituted for grape. It is used as a spread on scones, tea biscuits, English muffins or tea breads and as a glaze for, or accompaniment to, pork dishes, chicken or duck.

1 cup port wine
1 cup fresh grape juice (see page 41), or fine-quality
  commercially canned grape juice
3½ cups sugar
½ 6-ounce bottle liquid pectin

Place wine and juice with the sugar in a heavy saucepan. Bring to a boil over medium heat. Stir constantly until sugar is completely dissolved. Remove from the heat and stir in liquid pectin. Skim off foam with metal spoon and immediately pour into hot sterilized jars, cap and process for 10 minutes in a boiling water bath as directed on pages 30–32.

HORSERADISH JELLY

QUANTITY	THREE ½-PINT JARS
METHOD & SHELF LIFE	WATER BATH − 1 YEAR REFRIGERATION − 6 WEEKS

One of my favorite jellies comes from a fine old English recipe also used by the Shakers. This jelly is primarily used as a garnish for cold beef, meat salads or pot roast.

1 cup grated fresh horseradish
1 cup white wine vinegar
¼ teaspoon minced fresh sage
3¼ cups sugar
½ cup liquid pectin

Place horseradish, vinegar and sage in a heavy saucepan. Stir in the sugar. Cook over high heat, stirring constantly, until mixture comes to a hard boil. Add liquid pectin and again bring to a full boil. Boil for 1 minute. Remove from the heat and skim off foam with metal spoon. Immediately pour into hot sterilized jars. Cap and process for 10 minutes in a boiling water bath as directed on pages 30-32.

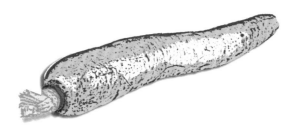

CASSIS JELLY

QUANTITY	FOUR ½-PINT JARS
METHOD & SHELF LIFE	WATER BATH – 1 YEAR REFRIGERATION – 6 WEEKS

This perfect garnish for poultry and game is a gourmet re-placement in all desserts, sauces or glazes calling for currant jelly.

3 cups fresh currant juice, or fresh cranberry-apple juice
  (see page 41), or fine-quality commercially canned
  unprocessed juice, strained
1 cup cassis liqueur
2 tablespoons fresh lemon juice
3¼ cups sugar
½ 6-ounce bottle liquid pectin

Place currant juice (or cranberry-apple juice), cassis and lemon juice in a heavy saucepan over high heat. Stir in the sugar and bring to a boil, stirring constantly. Add liquid pectin and, stirring constantly, cook until mixture comes to a full, rolling boil. Boil for 1 minute. Remove from the heat and skim off foam with metal spoon. Immediately pour into hot sterilized jars, cap and process for 10 minutes in a boiling water bath as directed on pages 30–32.

HERB OR MINT JELLIES

QUANTITY	FOUR ½-PINT JARS
METHOD & SHELF LIFE	WATER BATH – 1 YEAR REFRIGERATION – 6 WEEKS

Herb jellies are primarily used for meat or poultry garnish. I use them on pumpernickel tea sandwiches with a thin spread of sweet butter, fresh goat cheese or another soft, pungent cheese.

1 cup finely chopped fresh mint (stems and leaves) or sage (stems and leaves) or marjoram (stems and leaves) or tarragon (stems and leaves) or basil (stems and leaves), preferably organic
1 cup boiling water
3 cups sugar
½ cup cider vinegar
1 teaspoon fresh lemon juice
½ 6-ounce bottle liquid pectin
Green food coloring (optional)
4 sprigs of the herb used (optional)

Place the chopped fresh mint or herb in a heat-resistant bowl. Add 1 cup boiling water, cover and let stand for 30 minutes. Strain liquid through cheesecloth and add enough water to make 1 cup. Combine the herb infusion with the sugar, vinegar and lemon juice in a heavy saucepan. Place over high heat and cook until the mixture comes to a boil. Immediately add liquid pectin and food coloring, if desired, and continue cooking until mixture comes to a full, rolling boil. Boil for exactly 1 minute. Remove from the heat and skim off foam with metal spoon. Immediately pour into hot sterilized jars, add herb sprigs if desired. Cap and process for 10 minutes in a boiling water bath as directed on pages 30-32.

ORANGE SAUTERNE JELLY

QUANTITY   SIX ½-PINT JARS

METHOD   WATER BATH – 1 YEAR
&   REFRIGERATION – 6 WEEKS
SHELF LIFE

Sauterne may be replaced by other white wines in this sweet-tart jelly. The flavor lends itself for use both as a spread on breads and as a meat glaze. It can also be reheated for use as a dessert sauce on ice cream, sliced oranges or berries.

3½ cups fresh orange juice, strained
1½ cups good-quality Sauterne
1 teaspoon fresh lemon juice
3¼ cups sugar
1 box powdered light fruit pectin
6 sprigs of fresh tarragon (optional)

Place orange juice, Sauterne and lemon juice in a heavy saucepan. Mix together ¾ cup sugar and the powdered light fruit pectin. Add to wine mixture. Cook over high heat, stirring constantly until mixture comes to a hard boil. Stir in remaining sugar. Bring to a rolling boil, stirring constantly. Boil for 1 minute. Remove from the heat and skim off foam with metal spoon. Immediately pour into hot sterilized jars, cap and process for 10 minutes in a boiling water bath as directed on pages 30-32.

GINGER APPLE JELLY

QUANTITY   FIVE ½-PINT JARS

METHOD   WATER BATH – 1 YEAR
   &   REFRIGERATION – 6 WEEKS
SHELF LIFE

A special tangy jelly used as a replacement for the multi-purpose apple jelly in sauces, desserts and glazes.

4 cups fresh apple juice (see page 41), or fine-quality,
  commercially-canned, unprocessed apple juice, strained
3 tablespoons grated fresh ginger
1 teaspoon fresh lemon juice
3 cups sugar
1 box powdered light fruit pectin

Place apple juice and ginger in a heavy saucepan over high heat. Bring to a boil. Immediately remove from the heat, cover and let stand for 1 hour. Strain the apple mixture through a fine mesh sieve to remove ginger particles. Add lemon juice and transfer to a heavy saucepan. Place over high heat. Mix together ¾ cup sugar and the powdered light fruit pectin and stir it into the juice. Bring the mixture to a hard boil, stirring constantly. Stir in the remaining 2¼ cups sugar. Bring to a rolling boil, stirring constantly. Boil for 1 minute. Immediately remove from the heat, skim off foam with metal spoon and pour into hot sterilized jars. Cap and process for 10 minutes in a boiling water bath as directed on pages 30-32.

CHAMPAGNE JELLY

QUANTITY	FOUR ½-PINT JARS
METHOD & SHELF LIFE	WATER BATH – 1 YEAR REFRIGERATION – 6 WEEKS

A wonderful bite to spread on tea breads, scones or biscuits. Champagne Jelly is also a superb coating on white or pound cake, to be covered with a bittersweet chocolate glaze. Or try it as a glaze on broiled fruits for a brunch treat.

2 cups fine quality champagne
1 teaspoon fresh lemon juice, strained
2 tablespoons powdered pectin
3 cups sugar

Combine the champagne and lemon juice in a heavy saucepan over high heat. Stir in the powdered pectin and cook, stirring constantly until mixture comes to a boil. Quickly stir in the sugar. Cook, stirring constantly until mixture reaches full, rolling boil. Immediately remove from the heat, skim off foam with metal spoon and pour into hot sterilized jars. Cap and process for 10 minutes in a boiling water bath as directed on pages 30-32.

FRAMBOISE JELLY

QUANTITY	FOUR ½-PINT JARS
METHOD & SHELF LIFE	WATER BATH – 1 YEAR REFRIGERATION – 6 WEEKS

The combination of the delicacy of fresh raspberries and the mellow framboise (raspberry liqueur) makes a truly remarkable jelly. Use both as a spread and as a dessert garnish.

4½ cups fresh raspberries, preferably organic
3 cups sugar
¼ cup *framboise* or other raspberry-flavored liqueur

Place the raspberries, sugar and *framboise* in a heavy saucepan over medium heat. Bring to a boil, stirring occasionally. When mixture comes to a boil, raise the heat to high and cook, stirring constantly for about 20 minutes. As mixture begins to thicken, watch carefully to prevent sticking. When mixture has reached a jam-like consistency, immediately remove from the heat. Pour into hot sterilized jars, cap and process for 10 minutes in a boiling water bath as directed on pages 30-32.

SPICED TOMATO JAM

QUANTITY   FOUR ½-PINT JARS

METHOD   WATER BATH – 1 YEAR
&   REFRIGERATION – 6 WEEKS
SHELF LIFE

This jam was an early American favorite — a way to use the bounty of the late summer tomato crop. Spiced tomato jam can also be made with green, yellow or plum tomatoes and may be used both as a spread and as a glaze or as an accompaniment to meat or poultry.

3½ cups peeled and chopped fresh, ripe tomatoes OR
   canned tomatoes, drained and chopped, preferably
   organic
3 teaspoons fresh lemon juice
Grated zest of 1 lemon, preferably organic
½ teaspoon ground cinnamon
¼ teaspoon ground mace
¼ teaspoon ground ginger
3 cups sugar
1 box powdered light fruit pectin
4 cinnamon sticks

Mix together ¾ cup sugar and the powdered light fruit pectin. Place the tomatoes, lemon juice and zest, cinnamon, mace and ginger in a heavy saucepan over high heat. Cook, stirring constantly until mixture comes to a hard boil. Stir in remaining 2¼ cups sugar. Bring to a rolling boil, stirring constantly. Boil for 1 minute. Remove from the heat and skim off foam with metal spoon. Immediately pour into hot sterilized jars and add 1 cinnamon stick per jar. Cap and process for 10 minutes in a boiling water bath as directed on pages 30-32.

MARYELLA MIXON'S WINTER BLUEBERRY JAM

QUANTITY   FOUR ½-PINT JARS

METHOD   WATER BATH – 1 YEAR
&   REFRIGERATION – 6 WEEKS
SHELF LIFE

My dear friend Aris Mixon's late mom, Maryella, provided me with many wonderful recipes over the years. Her fine Southern hospitality was renowned; her table always groaned with fine food and her pantry was always full of homemade treats. This was her way of bringing summer to the winter table as blueberries are the one fruit that freezes beautifully.

1 cup chopped tart green apples (such as Granny Smith),
   preferably organic
1 lemon, preferably organic, seeded and chopped
1 pint frozen blueberries, preferably organic
3 cups sugar
½ cup water

Place apples and lemon in bowl of food processor fitted with the metal blade. Using quick on-and-off turns, process until finely chopped. Scrape the apple mixture into a large saucepan. Add the blueberries along with the sugar and water and bring to a boil. Cook, stirring constantly until the blueberries thaw and the sugar dissolves. Boil gently, uncovered, stirring occasionally, for about 30 minutes. When jam has thickened, remove from the heat. Immediately pour into hot sterilized jars, cap and process for 10 minutes in a boiling water bath as directed on pages 30-32.

BLACKBERRY BRANDY JAM

QUANTITY	FOUR ½-PINT JARS
METHOD & SHELF LIFE	WATER BATH – 1 YEAR REFRIGERATION – 6 WEEKS

A perfect blending of fresh blackberries and brandy makes a jam that can be used as a fine preserve or a spread or as a topping for ice cream or cake. It can be used whenever a fine preserve is required.

4½ cups fresh blackberries, preferably organic
3 teaspoons fresh lemon juice
3 cups sugar
¼ cup blackberry brandy

Combine blackberries and lemon juice in a heavy saucepan over medium heat. Stir in the sugar and bring to a boil, stirring frequently. Raise the heat and cook, stirring constantly for about 20 minutes. Add brandy. Cook for an additional 10 minutes or until mixture begins to thicken.

Remove from the heat and skim off foam with metal spoon. Immediately pour into hot sterilized jars, cap and process for 10 minutes in a boiling water bath as directed on pages 30-32.

FRESH FIG JAM

QUANTITY   FOUR ½-PINT JARS

METHOD   WATER BATH – 1 YEAR
&   REFRIGERATION – 6 WEEKS
SHELF LIFE

I generally have difficulty gathering enough figs to make jam, as ripe figs and cheese together make one of my favorite snacks, with a glass of wine, of course! Whenever you can gather enough to make this jam, do so. Not only is it a great spread, it is a perfect filling for cookies and cakes.

4 cups chopped fresh figs, preferably organic
¼ cup fresh lemon juice
Grated zest of 1 lemon, preferably organic
3 cups sugar
½ cup water
¼ teaspoon ground cinnamon

Combine the figs with the lemon juice and zest in a heavy saucepan over medium heat. Stir in the sugar, water and cinnamon and bring to a boil, stirring frequently. When mixture has reached the boiling point, raise the heat and cook for approximately 20 minutes, stirring frequently until mixture has thickened. Watch to prevent scorching. Remove from the heat. Immediately pour into hot sterilized jars, cap and process for 10 minutes in a boiling water bath as directed on pages 30-32.

BASIL JAM

QUANTITY	FOUR ½-PINT JARS
METHOD & SHELF LIFE	WATER BATH – 1 YEAR REFRIGERATION – 6 WEEKS

A new twist to a favorite combination. This pungent jam can be used as a spread as well as an accompaniment to meats and poultry.

3 cups sugar
1 box powdered light fruit pectin
3½ cups cooked, seeded and chopped fresh tomatoes,
   preferably organic
¾ cup chopped fresh basil (stems and leaves),
   preferably organic
¼ cup lemon juice

Mix ¾ cup sugar and the powdered light fruit pectin together in a small bowl. Combine the tomatoes, basil and lemon juice in a heavy saucepan. Stir in the sugar/pectin mixture and place over high heat. Bring to a full, rolling boil, stirring constantly. Stir in the remaining 2¼ cups sugar. Again, bring mixture to a full, rolling boil. Boil, stirring constantly, for 1 minute. Immediately remove from the heat and skim off foam with metal spoon. Pour at once into hot sterilized jars, cap and process for 10 minutes in a boiling water bath as directed on pages 30-32.

PENNSYLVANIA PEACH JAM

QUANTITY	SIX ½-PINT JARS
METHOD & SHELF LIFE	WATER BATH – 1 YEAR REFRIGERATION – 6 WEEKS

I don't know why this is called Pennsylvania Peach Jam but I assume it was devised by the wonderful folks in the Pennsylvania Dutch country, where peaches are even more luscious than those famous Georgia gems.

3 cups sugar
1 box powdered light fruit pectin
4 cups chopped fresh peaches, preferably organic
1½ cups fresh orange juice
1 teaspoon lemon juice
Grated zest of 1 orange, preferably organic
1 bottle maraschino cherries, drained and cut in half

Mix together ¾ cup sugar and the powdered light fruit pectin in a small bowl. Combine the peaches, orange juice, lemon juice and zest in a heavy saucepan over high heat. Stir in the sugar/pectin mixture and cook over high heat, stirring constantly, until mixture comes to a hard boil. Stir in the remaining 2¼ cups sugar and bring to a rolling boil, stirring constantly. Boil for 1 minute. Remove from the heat and skim off foam with metal spoon. Stir in the cherries and immediately pour into hot sterilized jars, cap and process for 10 minutes in a boiling water bath as directed on pages 30–32.

STRAWBERRY GRAND-MARNIER JAM

QUANTITY   FOUR ½-PINT JARS

METHOD   WATER BATH – 1 YEAR
&   REFRIGERATION – 6 WEEKS
SHELF LIFE

This is a wonderful jam to use as a jelly roll filling and, of course, as a spread on all tea breads, scones and muffins.

4½ cups fresh strawberries, preferably organic,
  well-washed and hulled
3 cups sugar
1¼ cup Grand Marnier or other orange-flavored liqueur

Place strawberries and sugar in a heavy saucepan over medium heat. Bring to a boil, stirring constantly. Raise the heat and cook for about 30 minutes or until mixture reaches a jam-like consistency. Remove from the heat and quickly stir in the Grand Marnier. Immediately pour into hot sterilized jars, cap and process for 10 minutes in a boiling water bath as directed on pages 30-32.

ANNIE McDONAGH'S
RHUBARB GINGER JAM

QUANTITY	FIVE ½-PINT JARS
METHOD & SHELF LIFE	WATER BATH — 1 YEAR REFRIGERATION — 6 WEEKS

Both rhubarb and ginger were early American favorites brought from the British Isles, where the zesty flavor of ginger was (and still is) used frequently as a dessert enhancer. (Rhubarb has historically been a favorite English and Irish dessert fruit.) This recipe was given to me by my Irish-speakin' almost-daughter, Anne McDonagh.

4 cups sugar
1 box powdered light fruit pectin
4 cups cooked, chopped rhubarb, preferably organic
1 tablespoon grated fresh ginger
1 tablespoon fresh lemon juice
¼ cup peeled and chopped ginger (you can also use
  candied ginger, if you wish a less pungent flavor)

Mix together ¾ cup sugar and the powdered light fruit pectin in a small bowl. Combine the rhubarb, grated ginger and lemon juice in a heavy saucepan over high heat. Stir in the sugar/pectin mixture and cook, stirring constantly until mixture comes to a hard boil. Stir in remaining 2¼ cups sugar and bring to a rolling boil, stirring constantly. Boil for 1 minute. Remove from the heat and stir in the chopped ginger. Skim off foam with metal spoon. Immediately pour into hot sterilized jars, cap and process for 10 minutes in a boiling water bath as directed on pages 30–32.

SAMBUCA ROMANA JAM

QUANTITY	FOUR ½-PINT JARS
METHOD & SHELF LIFE	WATER BATH — 1 YEAR REFRIGERATION — 6 WEEKS

Don't forget to add the coffee beans, which give the finished jam its extra-special coffee flavor. This jam makes a dramatic topping on lemon sorbet with the beans to be nibbled with espresso.

2½ cups sugar
1 box powdered light fruit pectin
5 cups crushed, fresh blueberries, preferably organic
1 teaspoon freshly grated lemon zest, preferably organic
½ cup water
½ cup Sambuca Romana or other coffee-flavored liqueur
10 coffee beans per jar

Mix ¾ cup sugar and the powdered light fruit pectin together in a small bowl. Combine the blueberries and lemon zest in a heavy saucepan. Stir in the water and Sambuca along with the sugar/pectin mixture and place over high heat. Bring to a hard boil, stirring constantly. Stir in the remaining 1¾ cups sugar. Bring to a rolling boil, still stirring constantly. Boil for 1 minute. Remove from the heat. Skim off foam with metal spoon. Place 10 coffee beans in each jar. Immediately pour jam into hot sterilized jars, cap and process for 10 minutes in a boiling water bath as directed on pages 30-32.

BAR-LE-DUC JAM

QUANTITY	FOUR ½-PINT JARS
METHOD & SHELF LIFE	WATER BATH – 1 YEAR REFRIGERATION – 6 WEEKS

Named for the town in France that is famous for its red currant jams, this is the jam most frequently called for in fine French cooking and pastry making. It is also often used as a condiment with roasted wild game.

8 cups whole red currants, preferably organic
1 tablespoon fresh lemon juice
6 cups sugar

Combine currants and lemon juice with 4 cups of the sugar in a heavy saucepan over medium heat. Bring to a boil, stirring frequently. Continue to boil for 5 minutes, stirring constantly. Remove from the heat, cover and let stand in a cool place for 12 hours. Place over medium heat and add remaining sugar. Cook, stirring constantly, until sugar dissolves. Raise the heat and bring to a full, rolling boil, then lower the heat to a low boil. Stirring frequently, cook for about 30 minutes or until jam is very thick.

Immediately pour into hot sterilized jars, cap and process for 10 minutes in a boiling water bath as directed on pages 30–32.

MOM'S SPECIAL
STRAWBERRY PRESERVES

QUANTITY   FOUR ½-PINT JARS

METHOD   WATER BATH — 1 YEAR
&   REFRIGERATION — 6 WEEKS
SHELF LIFE

*Year after year, my mother made these old-fashioned preserves.
A bit sweet for today's taste, but as simple, as pure and as old a
recipe as you can find.*

1 quart medium-sized very ripe, fresh strawberries,
  preferably organic, well-washed and hulled
4 cups sugar
½ cup lemon juice

Mix berries and sugar together in glass bowl. Cover
and let stand overnight. In the morning, place the berry
mixture in a heavy saucepan over medium heat. Add
lemon juice and bring to a full, rolling boil. Boil for 5
minutes, stirring constantly.

Remove from the heat. Cover and let stand in a cool
place for 24 hours. Again bring to a boil. Remove from
the heat, immediately pour into hot sterilized jars, cap
and process for 10 minutes in a boiling water bath as
directed on pages 30-32.

KUMQUAT GRAND-MARNIER PRESERVES

QUANTITY	FOUR ½-PINT JARS
METHOD & SHELF LIFE	WATER BATH — 1 YEAR REFRIGERATION — 6 WEEKS

This is technically a marmalade, since you use the whole kumquat, but it is known throughout the South as a special winter preserve. I use it most frequently as an accompaniment to game.

4½ cups whole kumquats, preferably organic
2 quarts plus ½ cup cold water
2 teaspoons salt
3½ cups sugar
3 cups fresh orange juice
1 cup mild-flavored honey
¼ cup Grand Marnier or other orange-flavored liqueur

With a sterilized needle, make about 6 punctures in the skin of each kumquat. Place in glass bowl. Stir in 2 quarts water and 2 teaspoons salt. Cover and set aside for at least 12 hours or up to 24 hours. Drain well and then rinse with fresh water. Combine the drained kumquats with the sugar, orange juice, honey, Grand Marnier and remaining ½ cup of water in a heavy saucepan. Place over medium heat and bring to a boil. Cook for approximately 40 minutes or until mixture begins to be clear and quite thick.

Remove from the heat. Cover and let stand for 2 days in a cool spot. Uncover and place over high heat and bring to a boil. Immediately remove from the heat and pour into hot sterilized jars, cap and process for 10 minutes in a boiling water bath as directed on pages 30-32.

SHAKER GREEN TOMATO PRESERVES

QUANTITY   FOUR ½-PINT JARS

METHOD   WATER BATH – 1 YEAR
&   REFRIGERATION – 6 WEEKS
SHELF LIFE

It is not always easy to find green or unripe tomatoes unless you go directly to your own garden or a farm stand. But not only are they terrific fried, they make marvelous jam. I have updated this recipe to gel with less sugar than the old-fashioned preserve made by the Shakers. This jam is perfect for late, just-before-the-frost tomatoes.

3¼ cups chopped green tomatoes, preferably organic
1 teaspoon salt
1 lemon, preferably organic, seeded and chopped fine
2 tablespoons chopped preserved ginger
1 teaspoon ground cinnamon
¼ teaspoon ground nutmeg
¼ teaspoon ground allspice
1½ cups brown sugar
1 box powdered light fruit pectin

Place the chopped green tomatoes and salt in a nonreactive bowl and add cool water to cover them completely. Cover with a lid or a tight-fitting piece of aluminum foil or plastic film and set aside to soak for at least 6 hours. Drain and rinse with fresh water. Combine the drained tomatoes, lemon, ginger, cinnamon, nutmeg and allspice in heavy saucepan over medium heat. Combine ¾ cup of the sugar with the powdered light fruit pectin and stir it into the tomato mixture. Raise the heat to high and cook, stirring constantly, until mixture comes to a hard boil. Stir in the remaining ¾ cup of sugar and bring to a rolling boil, stirring constantly. Boil for 1 minute. Remove from the heat. Skim off foam with metal spoon. Immediately pour into hot sterilized jars, cap and process for 10 minutes in a boiling water bath as directed on pages 30–32.

PURE RASPBERRY PRESERVES

QUANTITY	EIGHT ½-PINT JARS

METHOD & SHELF LIFE	WATER BATH – 1 YEAR REFRIGERATION – 6 WEEKS

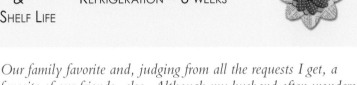

Our family favorite and, judging from all the requests I get, a favorite of our friends, also. Although my husband often wonders if the miles we drive to buy flats of fresh, perfect raspberries at an affordable price are really worth the difference in my canning budget. Yet, we do it year after year. I think you will join us once you get a taste!

4½ cups sugar
1 box powdered light fruit pectin
9 cups firm whole raspberries, preferably organic
1 tablespoon fresh lemon juice

Mix ¾ cup of the sugar with the powdered light fruit pectin in a small bowl. Combine the raspberries and lemon juice in a heavy saucepan. Stir in the sugar/pectin mixture and place over high heat. Quickly bring the fruit mixture to a full boil, stirring constantly. Stir in the remaining 3¾ cups of sugar and continuing to stir, bring to a full, rolling boil. Boil hard for 1 minute, stirring constantly. Remove from the heat and immediately pour into hot sterilized jars, cap and process for 10 minutes in a boiling water bath as directed on pages 30-32.

BLACK FOREST PRESERVES

QUANTITY	SIX ½-PINT JARS
METHOD & SHELF LIFE	WATER BATH — 1 YEAR REFRIGERATION — 6 WEEKS

A wonderful dessert topping or filling for a homemade Black Forest cake as well as a very special brunch treat when spread on toasted fresh rye bread slathered with cream cheese.

3¼ cups sugar
1 box powdered light fruit pectin
4½ cups pitted and halved fresh Bing cherries,
   preferably organic
¼ cup Kirschwasser or other cherry-flavored liqueur
1 teaspoon fresh lemon juice

Mix ¾ cup of the sugar with the powdered light fruit pectin in a small bowl. Combine the cherries, Kirschwasser and lemon juice in a heavy saucepan over medium heat. Bring to a boil, stirring constantly. When mixture comes to a hard boil, stir in remaining 2½ cups of sugar. Bring to a full, rolling boil, stirring constantly. Boil for 1 minute. Remove from the heat. Skim off foam with metal spoon. Immediately pour into hot sterilized jars, cap and process for 10 minutes in a boiling water bath as directed on pages 30-32.

PAPAYA LIME PRESERVES

QUANTITY   FOUR ½-PINT JARS

METHOD   WATER BATH – 1 YEAR
&   REFRIGERATION – 6 WEEKS
SHELF LIFE

The first exotic fruit I ever tasted in my first grown-up, fancy restaurant was papaya. Combined with lime, it makes an unforgettable flavor. Papaw may be used to replace papaya if it is native to your area.

2 cups water
2 cups sugar
¼ cup lime juice
Grated zest of 1 lime, preferably organic
¼ teaspoon ground cinnamon
2 cups peeled, seeded and chunked fresh papaya,
   preferably organic

Combine water, sugar, lime juice, zest and cinnamon in a heavy saucepan over medium heat. Bring to a boil and boil rapidly for 5 minutes. Stir in the papaya and again bring to a boil. Lower the heat and cook slowly for about 40 minutes, or until fruit is transparent. Remove from the heat, immediately pour into hot sterilized jars, cap and process for 10 minutes in a boiling water bath as directed on pages 30-32.

GINGER PEAR PRESERVES

QUANTITY   FIVE ½-PINT JARS

METHOD   WATER BATH – 1 YEAR
&   REFRIGERATION – 6 WEEKS
SHELF LIFE

I like to use this preserve mixed with whipped cream on fresh, warm gingerbread. It also makes a wonderful glaze on baked winter fruits.

6 cups cored and chunked hard, ripe pears,
  preferably organic
1 whole lemon, preferably organic, seeded and chopped
¼ cup grated fresh ginger (or chopped candied ginger,
  if preferred)
4 cups sugar
½ cup water
¼ cup Poire Williams or other pear-flavored liqueur

Combine the pears with the lemon and ginger in a heavy saucepan. Stir in the sugar, water and pear liqueur and bring to a boil. Lower the heat and simmer gently for 15 minutes. Remove from the heat, cover and let stand in a cool place for 12 hours. Return to high heat and bring to a boil. Cook at a soft boil, stirring constantly, for about 40 minutes or until thick and translucent. Remove from the heat and immediately pour into hot sterilized jars, cap and process for 10 minutes in a boiling water bath as directed on pages 30-32.

CHAPTER 4

CONSERVES, MARMALADES & BUTTERS

Conserves are made of combinations of several fruits or vegetables and usually contain nuts and raisins. They are cooked until thick and clear and of the consistency of jelly. Conserves are generally used as a condiment for meats or game.

Marmalades are made of thinly sliced or chopped fruits or vegetables and will usually contain some rind. The fruits or vegetables are combined with a relatively large proportion of sugar. Marmalades should also be cooked until the pieces of fruit or vegetable are clear and the mixture is the consistency of jelly.

When using citrus fruit, always use some of the white pith, as it is high in pectin. Try to use thin-skinned, untreated fruit, as it is much closer to its historical counterpart. Marmalades are used on tea breads, toast, scones, muffins, to top desserts or to glaze poultry, game or pork.

Butters are made of fruit that has been cooked until tender in just enough water to prevent sticking. The cooked fruit is run through a food processor, food mill or sieve and usually then combined with sugar. Spices are occasionally added for a robust flavor. A fruit butter is cooked slowly and stirred frequently until very thick. Butters are the purest form of cooked fruit and can be made with no sugar, if desired. One of my favorite uses of butters is as a coating on duck. The crisp, succulent skin is especially delicious with a crackling fruit butter coating.

All conserves, marmalades and butters are made by the water bath method in canning jars with rubber-edged lids and caps as directed on pages 30–32.

CONSERVES

Brandied Date Conserve • Cranberry Orange Conserve • Hot Tomato Conserve • Gumbo • Old Rummy • Basil Conserve

MARMALADES

Red Onion Marmalade • Microwave Marmalade • Carrot Marmalade • Our Marmalade • Grand-Marnier Marmalade • Pumpkin Ginger Marmalade

BUTTERS

Apple-Brandy Butter • Perfect Apple Butter • Bourbon Butter • Ginger Pear Butter

BRANDIED DATE CONSERVE

QUANTITY   FOUR ½-PINT JARS

METHOD   WATER BATH — 1 YEAR
    &   REFRIGERATION — 6 WEEKS
SHELF LIFE   MAY BE FROZEN

A perfect filling stirred into whipped cream for cakes or sandwich cookies, a tasty topping for light cakes, and, of course, a rich garnish for meats and game, particularly pork.

2½ cups chopped dates
2 cups dried currants
1 cup brown sugar
½ cup fresh orange juice
3 tablespoons fresh lemon juice
½ cup water
½ cup very good brandy
½ cup chopped walnuts (or whatever nut you prefer)

Combine dates, currants, brown sugar, orange juice and lemon juice in a heavy saucepan. Stir in the water and place over medium heat. Bring to a boil. Lower the heat and cook, stirring frequently for 5 minutes. Remove from the heat and stir in the brandy and nuts. Immediately pour into hot sterilized jars, cap and process for 10 minutes in a boiling water bath as directed on pages 30-32.

CRANBERRY ORANGE CONSERVE

QUANTITY	SIX ½-PINT JARS

METHOD & SHELF LIFE	WATER BATH — 1 YEAR
	REFRIGERATION — 6 WEEKS
	MAY BE FROZEN

Always on our table at Thanksgiving and Christmas, but a tasty garnish for meats, poultry and game all year long. I like to add a cup of Cranberry Orange Conserve to the batter when I make a pound cake.

1 whole orange, preferably organic, seeded and
  finely chopped
1½ cups white sugar
1 cup fresh orange juice
4 cups whole cranberries, preferably organic
1 cup brown sugar
1 cup raisins, preferably organic
1½ cups chopped pecans

Combine the chopped orange, white sugar and orange juice in a heavy saucepan over medium heat. Cook for approximately 20 minutes, or until orange peel is soft. Add cranberries, brown sugar and raisins. Cook until the mixture comes to a boil, stirring frequently. Lower heat and cook at a low boil for about 10 minutes, stirring constantly, until mixture thickens. Remove from heat and stir in pecans. Immediately pour into hot sterilized jars, cap and process for 10 minutes in a boiling water bath as directed on pages 30-32.

HOT TOMATO CONSERVE

QUANTITY	FOUR ½-PINT JARS

METHOD & SHELF LIFE	WATER BATH – 1 YEAR REFRIGERATION – 6 WEEKS MAY BE FROZEN

A touch of Tex-Mex flavors updates this old-fashioned red tomato conserve. I invented this when I had too many yellow tomatoes (purchased at a bargain price, of course). We love it. Yellow tomatoes have a delicate flavor all their own, and the conserve is only enhanced by the chilies.

5 cups halved small yellow tomatoes, preferably organic
2 jalapeño (or serrano) chilies, preferably organic,
   seeded and finely chopped
1 whole lemon, preferably organic, seeded and
   finely chopped
1 cup yellow raisins, preferably organic
1 tablespoon grated fresh orange zest, preferably organic
1 cup light brown sugar
1 cup white sugar
½ cup unsalted butter, at room temperature
1 cup toasted pumpkin seeds

Combine the tomatoes with the chilies, lemon, raisins and orange zest in a heavy saucepan. Stir in the sugars and butter and place over medium heat. Bring to a boil, stirring frequently. Lower heat, cover and let simmer for about 1 hour, stirring frequently to prevent sticking. When mixture has thickened, remove from heat, stir in toasted pumpkin seeds and immediately pour into hot sterilized jars. Cap and process for 10 minutes in a boiling water bath as directed on pages 30-32.

GUMBO CONSERVE

QUANTITY   SIX ½-PINT JARS

METHOD   WATER BATH – 1 YEAR
&   REFRIGERATION – 6 WEEKS
SHELF LIFE   MAY BE FROZEN

Why plum conserves are called gumbo in many traditional recipes, I don't know. Name notwithstanding, the preserves are delicious, either as a dessert or as a meat accompaniment.

5 cups chopped, pitted plums, preferably organic
2 cups chopped and seeded whole oranges,
 preferably organic
3 cups light brown sugar
1 cup raisins, preferably organic
1 tablespoon fresh lemon juice
½ teaspoon ground cinnamon
¼ teaspoon ground cloves
1 cup whole nut pieces

Combine the plums and oranges in the bowl of food processor fitted with the metal blade. Process until coarsely chopped. Combine the chopped fruit with the sugar, raisins, lemon juice, cinnamon and cloves in a heavy saucepan. Place over medium heat and bring to a boil, stirring frequently. Lower the heat and cook at a low boil for about 20 minutes, stirring frequently to prevent scorching. When mixture has thickened, remove from the heat and stir in nutmeats. Immediately pour into hot sterilized jars, cap and process for 10 minutes in a boiling water bath as directed on pages 30-32.

OLD RUMMY

QUANTITY   FOUR ½-PINT JARS

METHOD   WATER BATH — 1 YEAR
&   REFRIGERATION — 6 WEEKS
SHELF LIFE   MAY BE FROZEN

A family favorite — we first made this with fresh fruit while vacationing in the Caribbean. Piña coladas *are, of course, its inspiration. It makes a great base for homemade ice cream!*

1 large fresh pineapple, preferably organic,
  peeled and chopped
1 whole lemon, preferably organic, seeded and chopped
1 whole orange, preferably organic, seeded and chopped
1 cup grated fresh coconut, preferably organic
4 cups sugar
1 cup good white wine

Combine the pineapple with the lemon, orange and coconut in a heavy saucepan. Stir in the sugar and wine and place over medium heat. Bring to a boil. Lower the heat and cook for 20 minutes. Remove from heat and immediately pour into hot sterilized jars, cap and process for 10 minutes in a boiling water bath as directed on pages 30-32.

BASIL CONSERVE

QUANTITY	FOUR ½-PINT JARS

METHOD & SHELF LIFE	WATER BATH – 1 YEAR REFRIGERATION – 6 WEEKS MAY BE FROZEN

I can never have too much basil. I use every piece I can get: The large woody plants go into flower arrangements, and my sauté pan gets the new tender shoots with garlic and oil for use on pasta. This conserve is absolutely wonderful with grilled meats and fish.

1 whole lemon, preferably organic, seeded and chopped
4 cups chopped green tomatoes, preferably organic
3 cups chopped fresh basil (stems and leaves),
   preferably organic
3 cups sugar
1 cup dry white wine
1½ cups toasted pine nuts

Combine the lemon, tomatoes and basil in a heavy saucepan. Stir in the sugar and wine and place over medium heat. Bring to a boil. Lower the heat and simmer for about 30 minutes, stirring frequently. When mixture has begun to thicken, remove from heat and stir in toasted pine nuts. Immediately pour into hot sterilized jars, cap and process for 10 minutes in a boiling water bath as directed on pages 30-32.

RED ONION MARMALADE

QUANTITY	FOUR ½-PINT JARS
METHOD & SHELF LIFE	WATER BATH — 1 YEAR REFRIGERATION — 6 WEEKS MAY BE FROZEN

I clipped this recipe from a magazine (which one is long forgotten) to use for a cookout featuring grilled lime-marinated pork. It was such a hit that I have since expanded and added to it, and it is always on my winter preserves shelf.

8 cups peeled, quartered and sliced red onions
½ cup peeled and chopped shallots
½ cup light brown sugar
1 cup dry red wine
½ cup orange blossom honey
¼ cup balsamic vinegar
¼ cup virgin olive oil
1 tablespoon chopped fresh sage
1 tablespoon fresh ground black pepper

Place onion, shallots and brown sugar in a heavy saucepan over low heat, stirring frequently until mixture begins to caramelize and turn a light brown color. Stir in the wine, honey, vinegar, olive oil, sage and pepper. Continue to cook over low heat, stirring frequently to prevent scorching, for about 45 minutes or until mixture is a thick syrup. Immediately remove from the heat and pour into hot sterilized jars, cap and process for 10 minutes in a boiling water bath as directed on pages 30-32.

MICROWAVE MARMALADE

QUANTITY	ABOUT 1 CUP
METHOD & SHELF LIFE	MICROWAVE OVEN REFRIGERATION — 1 WEEK

I got this recipe from a readers' forum in a national food magazine. I can't remember which magazine or the contributor's name, but I do thank her. I've made this marmalade from all kinds of citrus fruit. It really works. And it is certainly the quickest and easiest preserve I've ever come across.

1 large organic orange, seeded (or 1 large grapefruit,
   or 2 large lemons or 2 large limes)
Sugar to equal fruit

Coarsely chop the orange (or grapefruit, lemons or limes) in the bowl of food processor fitted with the metal blade. Measure or weigh the fruit and transfer to a microwave bowl. Add an equal amount of sugar to the fruit. Stir to mix. Place in the center of a microwave oven. Cook on medium heat, stirring twice, for about 6 minutes or until syrup thickens. Do not overcook. Remove from oven, pour into sterilized container, cover and refrigerate until ready to use.

CARROT MARMALADE

QUANTITY   FIVE ½-PINT JARS

METHOD   WATER BATH – 1 YEAR
&   REFRIGERATION – 6 WEEKS
SHELF LIFE   MAY BE FROZEN

This is the first traditional Shaker recipe I ever tried. I think that it is delicious used either as a spread or a glaze.

3 cups cooked, chopped carrots, preferably organic
2 whole lemons, preferably organic, seeded and chopped
1 whole orange, preferably organic, seeded and chopped
4 cups sugar
1 tablespoon ground cinnamon

Combine the carrots with the lemons and orange in a heavy saucepan over medium heat. Stir in the sugar and cinnamon and bring to a boil, stirring frequently. Lower the heat and cook at a low simmer for about 30 minutes. When mixture begins to gel, remove from heat and immediately pour into hot sterilized jars. Cap and process for 10 minutes in a boiling water bath as directed on pages 30-32.

OUR MARMALADE

QUANTITY	FIVE ½-PINT JARS
METHOD & SHELF LIFE	WATER BATH — 1 YEAR REFRIGERATION — 6 WEEKS

My Scottish grandmother made it, my mother made it and I make it. Its simplicity makes it truly a gourmet preserve.

3 whole oranges, preferably organic, seeded and chopped
3 whole lemons, preferably organic, seeded and chopped
Water to equal chopped fruit
Sugar to equal cooked fruit

Measure chopped fruit in cups (or weigh it) and place in a heavy saucepan. Measure an equal amount of water and pour into the saucepan. Place over high heat and bring to a boil. Lower the heat and simmer for 5 minutes. Remove from the heat, cover and let stand in a cool place for 24 hours. Return to high heat, bring to a boil and boil for 10 minutes. Remove from the heat, cover and let stand in a cool place for another 24 hours. Measure out the fruit mixture and return to a clean, heavy saucepan. Measure an equal amount of sugar to the fruit and pour into saucepan. Place over medium-high heat and bring to a boil. Cook, stirring constantly for another 15 minutes or until mixture begins to gel. Remove from heat and immediately pour into hot jars, cap and process for 10 minutes in a boiling water bath as directed on pages 30-32.

GRAND-MARNIER MARMALADE

QUANTITY	SIX ½-PINT JARS
METHOD & SHELF LIFE	WATER BATH — 1 YEAR REFRIGERATION — 2 MONTHS

This sweet-tart marmalade is a wonderful glaze for game and poultry or a bittersweet glaze for a dense chocolate cake. Or, you can use just as you would plain orange marmalade.

2 cups thinly sliced kumquats, preferably organic
2 cups seeded and chopped whole navel oranges,
  preferably organic
7 cups water
¾ cup Grand Marnier or other orange-flavored liqueur
1 teaspoon freshly grated lemon zest, preferably organic
Sugar to equal cooked fruit

Combine the kumquats and oranges in a large nonreactive bowl. Add the water, cover and let stand in a cool place for 12 hours. Pour the soaked fruit along with the liquid into medium saucepan. Place over high heat and bring to a full, rolling boil. Cook for about 15 minutes, stirring frequently. Remove from the heat and stir in the Grand Marnier and lemon zest. Measure or weigh this mixture and add an equal amount of sugar. Return to high heat and again bring to a boil. Lower the heat and cook, stirring frequently for about 30 minutes. When mixture begins to gel, remove from heat and immediately pour into hot sterilized jars. Cap and process for 10 minutes in a boiling water bath as directed on pages 30–32.

PUMPKIN GINGER MARMALADE

QUANTITY	SIX ½-PINT JARS
METHOD & SHELF LIFE	WATER BATH – 1 YEAR REFRIGERATION – 6 WEEKS MAY BE FROZEN

This is sometimes called pumpkin pickle, sometimes pumpkin chip. I have experimented with the recipe and am delighted with its outcome.

6 lemons, preferably organic
1 small pumpkin, preferably organic, peeled, seeded
  and sliced into thin ½-inch-square chips
¼ cup grated fresh ginger
1 cup sugar for each cup pumpkin

Juice the 6 lemons, separately reserving the juice and rinds. Measure or weigh the pumpkin chips. Combine the pumpkin chips with the lemon juice and ginger in a glass bowl. Measure sugar to equal the exact amount of pumpkin chips. Stir the sugar into the pumpkin mixture. Cover and let stand for 12 hours. Chop the reserved lemon rinds. Place them in a heavy saucepan and cover with water. Place over medium heat and cook for about 15 minutes or until tender. Drain and set aside. Place the pumpkin mixture in a heavy saucepan over high heat. Bring to a boil and boil for about 45 minutes to 1 hour or until pumpkin chips are translucent. Remove from the heat. Remove pumpkin pieces from the syrup and set aside. Return syrup to high heat and bring to rolling boil. Boil for 15 minutes or until slightly thickened. Stir in the pumpkin and lemon rind and return to a boil for exactly 5 minutes. Remove from heat and pour into hot sterilized jars. Cap and process for 10 minutes in a boiling water bath as directed on pages 30-32.

APPLE-BRANDY BUTTER

QUANTITY   SIX ½-PINT JARS

METHOD   WATER BATH – 1 YEAR
&   REFRIGERATION – 6 WEEKS
SHELF LIFE   MAY BE FROZEN

The best! Use as a glaze, a spread or even whipped with sweet dairy butter for a breakfast or brunch treat. Or, it's a very special coating on roasted wild game.

6 cups fresh unsweetened, unspiced applesauce,
   preferably organic
1 cup sugar
½ cup Calvados or other apple-flavored brandy
½ cup orange blossom honey
1 tablespoon ground cinnamon
¼ teaspoon ground cloves

Combine the applesauce with the sugar, brandy, honey, cinnamon and cloves in a heavy saucepan. Place over medium heat and bring to a boil, stirring frequently. Cook for about 15 minutes or until mixture begins to thicken. Remove from the heat and pour into hot sterilized jars, leaving ¼-inch headspace. Cap and process in a 10-minute boiling water bath as directed on pages 30-32.

PERFECT APPLE BUTTER

QUANTITY   FOUR ½-PINT JARS

METHOD   WATER BATH – 1 YEAR
&   REFRIGERATION – 3 WEEKS
SHELF LIFE MAY BE FROZEN

As pure as you can get – just apples and a touch of cinnamon, if desired. And it's great for many dieters since there is no sugar or salt. This very tasty spread can be used on breads or toasts or as a dessert topping.

6 cups peeled and sliced sweet apples (such as McIntosh),
  preferably organic
1 cup fresh apple cider, preferably organic
1 tablespoon ground cinnamon (optional)

Combine apples and cider in a heavy saucepan over medium heat. Cook, stirring frequently, until the mixture comes to a boil. Lower the heat and simmer, stirring frequently, for about 1 hour, or until apple slices have disintegrated and butter is thick. Remove from the heat. Stir in cinnamon, if using. Pour into hot sterilized jars, leaving ¼-inch headspace. Cap and process in a 10-minute boiling water bath as directed on pages 30-32.

BOURBON BUTTER

QUANTITY   FIVE ½-PINT JARS

METHOD   WATER BATH – 1 YEAR
&   REFRIGERATION – 6 WEEKS
SHELF LIFE   MAY BE FROZEN

This is a fancy, rich butter that can be used as a coating on meats or game or as a spread for tea breads. It also makes a terrific filling for light cakes.

5 cups fresh peach purée, preferably organic
1 cup good-quality bourbon
2 cups sugar
2 tablespoons chopped fresh mint

Combine the peaches and bourbon in a heavy saucepan. Stir in the sugar and mint and place over medium heat. Bring to a boil, stirring frequently. Lower the heat and simmer for about 30 minutes or until butter is thick. Remove from the heat. Pour into hot sterilized jars, leaving ¼-inch headspace. Cap and process in a 10-minute boiling water bath as directed on pages 30–32.

GINGER PEAR BUTTER

QUANTITY   FOUR ½-PINT JARS

METHOD   WATER BATH – 1 YEAR
   &   REFRIGERATION – 6 WEEKS
SHELF LIFE

The fresh ginger adds a bite to the richness of this fruit butter. A wonderful filling for crepes with some chopped fresh pear added.

8 cups cored and sliced pears, preferably organic
4 cups sugar
½ cup grated fresh ginger
½ cup fresh lime juice
1 teaspoon freshly grated lime zest
½ teaspoon chopped fresh sage

Place pears in a heavy saucepan over medium heat. Add about ½ cup water. Cook, stirring frequently until pears are just soft. Add water if necessary, a little at a time, to prevent sticking. When the pears are soft, remove from heat. Transfer the cooked pears to the bowl of food processor fitted with the metal blade and process until smooth. Transfer the pear puree to a heavy saucepan. Add the sugar, ginger, lime juice, lime zest and sage. Place over medium heat and bring to a boil. Lower the heat and cook, stirring frequently for about 30 minutes or until the butter is thick. Remove from heat and immediately pour into hot sterilized jars, leaving ¼-inch headspace. Cap and process in a 10 minute boiling water bath as directed on pages 30-32.

SPICED FRUITS & CHUTNEYS

Spiced fruits are whole fruits or, less frequently, uniform slices or pieces of fruit (either one type or mixed) that are cooked in a sweet, spicy syrup until plump. The fruit retains its shape but takes on some of the color of the spice. Also known as pickled fruits, they are usually served as an accompaniment to meat, poultry or game. Spiced fruits may also be used successfully as dessert.

Chutneys are a hot, spicy-sweet mixed chopped fruit or vegetable jam-pickle. They can be exceedingly spicy, but the degree may be adjusted to individual taste. Authentically served with Indian curries, chutneys are also compatible with meat, poultry and fish.

For fail-safe processing, spiced fruits and chutneys require a boiling water bath in canning jars with rubber-edged lids. Follow directions as described on pages 30-32.

Spiced fruits and chutneys may be refrigerated for short-term storage as well as frozen for a period of no longer than 1 year.

SPICED FRUITS

Peaches in Port Wine • Moroccan Oranges • Ginger Pears • Marrons Glacés • Spiced Cranberry Cassis • Spiced Cherries

CHUTNEYS

Tomato Chutney • Lemon Chutney • Onion Chutney • Rhubarb Chutney • Celery Apple Chutney • What I Think is Traditional Chutney

PEACHES IN PORT WINE

QUANTITY   FOUR PINT JARS

METHOD   WATER BATH – 1 YEAR
&   REFRIGERATION – 6 WEEKS
SHELF LIFE

Peaches in wine are a wonderful multipurpose preserve. Excellent as a condiment with roasted meats and super as a cold dessert served with delicate lace or butter cookies.

20 medium peaches, preferably organic, peeled
3 cups water
3 cups port
2½ cups sugar
2 tablespoons fresh lemon juice
Peel of 1 organic orange, preferably in one long strip
12 whole cloves
Four 4-inch cinnamon sticks
1 tablespoon whole white peppercorns

Combine the peaches with the water and port in a large nonreactive saucepan. Add the sugar, lemon juice and orange peel, stirring gently. Add the cloves, cinnamon sticks and peppercorns and place over medium heat. Bring to a boil. Lower the heat and simmer for 10 minutes. Remove from the heat. Immediately pack 5 peaches into each hot sterilized jar, covering with syrup to ¼-inch headspace. Make sure that each jar contains some peppercorns, cloves and a cinnamon stick. Cap and process in a 10-minute boiling water bath as directed on pages 30-32.

MOROCCAN ORANGES

QUANTITY   FOUR ½-PINT JARS

METHOD   WATER BATH – 1 YEAR
   &   REFRIGERATION – 1 WEEK
SHELF LIFE

These very aromatic oranges may be served cold as a dessert, with crisp greens as a salad or in whipped cream as a cake filling. They may also be glazed with a bit of sweet butter under the broiler for use as a condiment or garnish for poultry or lamb.

8 medium navel oranges, preferably organic, peeled
   and sliced
2 cups fresh orange juice
¼ cup orange blossom water
1 teaspoon freshly grated lemon zest
1 teaspoon ground cinnamon
Three 4-inch cinnamon sticks, broken into small pieces

Combine the oranges with the juice, orange blossom water, lemon zest and ground cinnamon in a heavy saucepan. Stir in the cinnamon sticks and place over medium heat. Bring to a boil. Remove from the heat and immediately pack into hot sterilized jars, covering with syrup to ¼-inch headspace. Cap and process for 12 minutes in a boiling water bath as directed on pages 30-32.

GINGER PEARS

QUANTITY	FOUR PINT JARS
METHOD & SHELF LIFE	WATER BATH – 1 YEAR REFRIGERATION – 6 WEEKS

These tiny whole pears make a superb dessert covered with ginger cream. They work equally well as a garnish for roasted meats, poultry and game. They are particularly good with roast goose.

4½ cups water
2 tablespoons fresh lemon juice
3 to 4 pounds firm Seckel pears (preferably organic)
  with stems
1 lemon, preferably organic, thinly sliced
1 cup peeled and thinly sliced fresh ginger
½ cup small pieces stick cinnamon
¼ cup whole cloves
2 cups dry white wine
1 cup white vinegar
½ cup apple juice
3 cups sugar

Combine 4 cups of the water with the lemon juice in large bowl. Working with one at a time, carefully peel the pears, leaving the stems intact. As each pear is peeled, put it into the acidulated water. This will prevent pears from turning brown. Tie lemon, ginger, cinnamon pieces and cloves into a cheesecloth bag. Combine the remaining ½ cup of water with the wine, vinegar and apple juice in a heavy saucepan. Stir in the sugar and then add the cheesecloth bag. Bring to a boil over medium heat. Lower the heat and cook for 10 minutes. Remove from the heat and drain well. Carefully dry each pear with paper towel.

A few at a time, add the pears to the simmering syrup. (Do not pack pears into the saucepan, as it will take them too long to cook, and they are more likely to be damaged.) Cook for 10 minutes. Carefully remove the pears and set them aside in a heatproof container with a lid. Continue cooking until all of the pears are cooked.

When all of the pears are cooked, pour the hot syrup over them. Cover and let stand in a cool place for at least 12 hours or up to 24 hours. Place the cooled pears in a single layer in a large saucepan. Add the syrup and bring to a boil over high heat.

Remove from the heat and immediately pack pears into hot sterilized jars, covering with boiling syrup leaving ¼-inch headspace. Cap and process for 15 minutes in a boiling water bath as directed on pages 30-32.

MARRONS GLACÉS

QUANTITY	SIX PINT JARS
METHOD & SHELF LIFE	WATER BATH – 1 YEAR REFRIGERATION – 6 WEEKS

This classically elegant French preserve is not at all uncommon in the American kitchen. I have also preserved other nuts in this manner — pecans, black walnuts, English walnuts and hazelnuts — for a delicious dessert.

5 pounds whole raw chestnuts [See NOTE.]
5 cups sugar
2 cups water
1 cup dry white wine
Two 4-inch long whole cinnamon sticks
One 2-inch piece vanilla bean
1 teaspoon ground cinnamon
½ cup good-quality brandy

NOTE: If you use dried or processed nuts, there is no need to cook them. Do not, however, use salted nuts.

Place the raw nuts in a large heavy saucepan. Cover with water and bring to a boil over high heat. Lower the heat and cook for 30 minutes. Drain, cool and peel the chestnuts. Set aside. Combine the sugar, water, wine, cinnamon sticks, vanilla bean and ground cinnamon in a heavy saucepan. Place over medium heat and bring to a boil. Boil for 5 minutes. Add the peeled chestnuts and again bring to a boil. Lower the heat and cook gently for about 30 minutes, or until chestnuts are transparent. Remove from the heat and let stand in a cool place for 12 hours. Return to high heat and again bring to a boil. Boil for 10 minutes. Add the brandy and again return to a boil. Immediately remove from heat and pour into hot sterilized jars. Cap and process for 10 minutes in a boiling water bath as directed on pages 30-32.

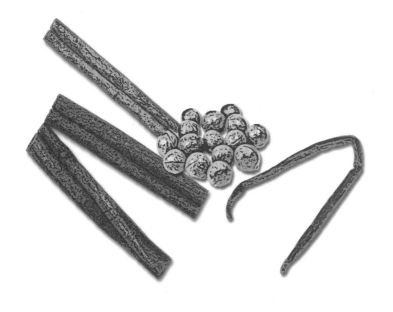

SPICED CRANBERRY CASSIS

QUANTITY   FIVE ½-PINT JARS

METHOD   WATER BATH – 1 YEAR
&   REFRIGERATION – 6 WEEKS
SHELF LIFE

This brings out the best in all poultry dishes — from roasts to cold salads. Over bittersweet chocolate ice cream, these cranberries make a sparkling dessert, especially if the sugar crystallizes, as it often does.

4 cups fresh cranberries, preferably organic, washed
  and dried
½ cup cider vinegar
¼ cup Crème de Cassis (black currant liqueur)
¼ cup water
2½ cups sugar
5 whole star anise
Two 4-inch cinnamon sticks, broken into pieces
1 tablespoon whole cloves

Combine the cranberries with the vinegar, cassis and water in a medium saucepan. Stir in the sugar and when blended, add the star anise, cinnamon sticks and cloves. Place over high heat and bring to a boil. Cook for 7 minutes. Remove from the heat and immediately pack into hot sterilized jars, making sure that each jar contains pieces of cinnamon stick, cloves and 1 star anise. Cap and process for 10 minutes in a boiling water bath as directed on pages 30-32.

SPICED CHERRIES

QUANTITY	FOUR ½-PINT JARS

METHOD & SHELF LIFE	NO PROCESSING REQUIRED REFRIGERATION – UP TO 1 YEAR

An old American favorite — my mom and aunts always had these on hand. Spiced cherries are an interesting garnish for meat and can also be used as a relish.

6 cups firm, ripe whole cherries, either sour or Bing
  (I prefer sour), preferably organic
Apple cider vinegar to cover fruit
Sugar to equal fruit
4 tablespoons ground cinnamon
½ teaspoon ground cloves
Four 2-inch cinnamon sticks

Place the cherries in glass bowl or crock with lid. Add enough apple cider vinegar to cover the fruit. Place the cover on the bowl and let stand in a cool, dark place for 3 days. Drain off the vinegar. Measure in cups (or weigh) the soaked cherries and return them to the crock. Add an equal amount of sugar to the fruit. Stir in the ground spices. Cover and let stand in a cool, dark place for 3 more days, turning the cherries over once each day. Pour into hot sterilized jars and add a stick of cinnamon to each. Cover tightly and refrigerate for at least 4 weeks before use.

TOMATO CHUTNEY

QUANTITY	EIGHT ½-PINT JARS
METHOD & SHELF LIFE	WATER BATH – 1 YEAR REFRIGERATION – 3 MONTHS MAY BE FROZEN

Try this updated version of an old favorite. This chutney might be a bit spicy for some but it can easily be adjusted to your taste by lessening the amounts of chili and cayenne pepper. I usually make it even hotter for my family's taste.

3 jalapeño chilies, preferably organic, seeded and chopped
4 cups peeled, cored and chopped red tomatoes,
  preferably organic
4 cups cored and chopped green tomatoes, preferably organic
4 cups peeled, cored and chopped green apples,
  preferably organic
2 cups chopped red onions, preferably organic
1 cup seedless raisins, preferably organic
½ cup seeded and chopped red bell peppers,
  preferably organic
½ cup seeded and chopped green bell peppers,
  preferably organic
¼ cup chopped fresh cilantro, preferably organic
2 tablespoons grated fresh ginger
1 tablespoon minced garlic
3 cups light brown sugar
3 cups apple cider vinegar
1 teaspoon cayenne pepper
1 teaspoon ground cinnamon
Salt to taste

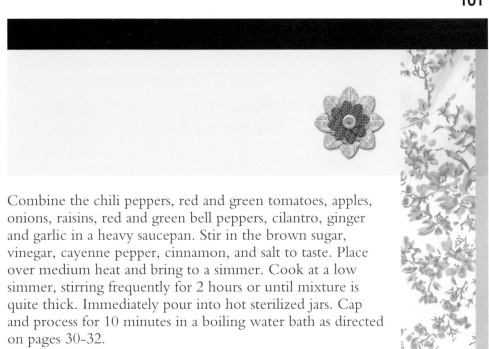

Combine the chili peppers, red and green tomatoes, apples, onions, raisins, red and green bell peppers, cilantro, ginger and garlic in a heavy saucepan. Stir in the brown sugar, vinegar, cayenne pepper, cinnamon, and salt to taste. Place over medium heat and bring to a simmer. Cook at a low simmer, stirring frequently for 2 hours or until mixture is quite thick. Immediately pour into hot sterilized jars. Cap and process for 10 minutes in a boiling water bath as directed on pages 30-32.

LEMON CHUTNEY

QUANTITY	FOUR ½-PINT JARS
METHOD & SHELF LIFE	WATER BATH – 1 YEAR REFRIGERATION – 2 MONTHS

This is my favorite chutney — tart but sweet, an interesting side dish with lamb.

2 cups cored and chopped Granny Smith apples, preferably organic
1½ cups seeded and chopped, preferably organic lemons
1 cup chopped, mixed dried fruit (no dates), preferably organic
1 cup golden raisins, preferably organic
½ cup chopped onions
1 teaspoon minced garlic
1 cup dry white wine
1 cup light brown sugar
½ cup granulated sugar
1 teaspoon whole mustard seeds
1 cup toasted pine nuts (or almonds)
¼ cup anisette or other anise-flavored liqueur

Combine the apples, lemon, dried fruit, raisins, onions and garlic in a heavy saucepan. Stir in the wine, brown and granulated sugars and mustard seeds. Place over medium heat and bring to a simmer. Cook at a gentle simmer for 30 minutes, stirring frequently. Do not boil. Remove from the heat. Stir in toasted pine nuts and anisette. Immediately pour into hot sterilized jars. Cap and process for 10 minutes in a boiling water bath as directed on pages 30-32.

ONION CHUTNEY

QUANTITY	FOUR ½-PINT JARS

METHOD & SHELF LIFE	WATER BATH — 1 YEAR REFRIGERATION — 3 MONTHS MAY BE FROZEN

This chutney is easy to make, easier to eat — a spicy onion garnish for meats, curries, stews or sandwiches.

6 cups chopped Vidalia onions
   (other sweet onions may be used), preferably organic
½ cup fresh lemon juice
¼ cup light brown sugar
2 teaspoons whole cumin seed
2 teaspoons ground chilies (not pre-prepared
   chili powder)
1 teaspoon whole mustard seed
½ teaspoon Tabasco sauce
¼ teaspoon red pepper flakes
Salt to taste

Combine the onions with the remaining ingredients in a heavy saucepan. Place over medium heat and bring to a boil, stirring frequently. When the mixture comes to a boil, immediately remove from heat and pack into hot sterilized jars. Cap and process for 10 minutes in a boiling water bath as directed on pages 30-32.

RHUBARB CHUTNEY

QUANTITY	FOUR ½-PINT JARS
METHOD & SHELF LIFE	WATER BATH – 1 YEAR REFRIGERATION – 3 MONTHS MAY BE FROZEN

A Victorian favorite updated by the use of red wine, this is an excellent garnish or condiment, particularly with roasted meats and wild game.

6 cups chopped rhubarb, preferably organic
1 large green apple, preferably organic, peeled,
  cored and chopped
1 cup chopped red onions, preferably organic
1 cup dried currants
½ cup peeled and chopped celery, preferably organic
1 tablespoon minced garlic
2½ cups light brown sugar
¾ cup dry red wine
1 teaspoon grated fresh ginger
1 teaspoon ground cinnamon
¼ teaspoon ground cloves

Combine the rhubarb with the apple, onions, currants, celery and garlic in a heavy saucepan. Stir in the brown sugar, red wine, ginger, cinnamon and cloves. Place over medium heat and bring to a boil, stirring frequently. Lower the heat and cook for about 30 minutes, or until mixture is thick. Immediately pour into hot sterilized jars. Cap and process for 10 minutes in a boiling water bath as directed on pages 30-32.

CELERY APPLE CHUTNEY

QUANTITY	SIX ½-PINT JARS
METHOD & SHELF LIFE	WATER BATH – 1 YEAR REFRIGERATION – 3 MONTHS

Crunchier than other chutneys with a lovely mustard flavor, and a terrific base for dressings used on mixed vegetables or meat or poultry salads.

6 cups peeled, cored and chopped green apples
1 medium red bell pepper, seeded and chopped
1 cup golden raisins
1 cup light brown sugar
½ cup chopped onions
¼ cup chopped candied ginger
3 tablespoons whole mustard seed
1 tablespoon minced garlic
½ cup white wine vinegar
1½ cups finely chopped celery

Combine the apples with the bell pepper, raisins, brown sugar, onions, ginger, mustard seed and garlic in a heavy saucepan. Stir in the vinegar and place over medium heat. Bring to a boil. Lower heat, cover and cook, stirring occasionally for about 25 minutes, or until mixture begins to thicken. Immediately add the celery and cook for an additional 5 minutes. Remove from heat and pour into hot sterilized jars. Cap and process for 10 minutes in a boiling water bath as directed on pages 30-32.

WHAT I THINK IS TRADITIONAL CHUTNEY

QUANTITY   FOUR ½-PINT JARS

METHOD   WATER BATH – 1 YEAR
  &   REFRIGERATION – 3 MONTHS
SHELF LIFE   MAY BE FROZEN

This is the closest I've been able to come to the tasty Major Grey's Chutney that is traditionally served with Indian curries. Although the original recipe is secret and, to my knowledge, never printed, I have used the same ingredients as those listed on the bottle.

4 cups peeled, seeded and sliced hard, ripe mango
1 cup chopped yellow onions
¾ cup yellow raisins
½ cup seeded and chopped lime
½ cup grated fresh ginger
1 tablespoon minced garlic
2 cups light brown sugar
1 cup apple cider vinegar
¼ cup fresh orange juice
¼ cup fresh lemon juice
1 tablespoon whole mustard seed
1 teaspoon dried red pepper flakes
1 teaspoon ground cinnamon
¼ teaspoon ground cloves

Combine the mango with the onions, raisins, lime, ginger and garlic in a heavy saucepan. Stir in the sugar, vinegar and orange and lemon juices along with the mustard seed, pepper flakes, cinnamon and cloves. Place over medium heat and bring to a boil. Lower the heat and simmer for

about 20 minutes, stirring frequently. Remove from the heat, cover and let stand for about 12 hours. Return the pan to medium heat and again bring to a boil. Lower the heat and cook for 15 minutes, stirring frequently. Remove from heat and immediately pour into hot sterilized jars. Cap and process for 10 minutes in a boiling water bath as directed on pages 30-32.

CHAPTER 6

RELISHES & PICKLES

Relishes are made of vegetables or fruits or a combination of vegetables and fruits. The vegetables and fruits used are finely sliced, shredded or chopped. Made with vinegar and spices and/ or herbs, relishes may be sweet or sour, spicy or mellow. Only recently rediscovered in all their glorious variety, they are used as accompaniments to meat, poultry or game and as a dressing on sandwiches or salads.

Pickles are also made of vegetables or fruit. They may be left whole, sliced, chopped or peeled according to the type of pickle desired. Vegetables may be pickled by the use of salt or vinegar, or by vinegar and salt in combination, often with added sugar. Fruits are pickled by the use of vinegar, sugar and spices. Whole spices should be tied in a thin cloth bag, usually cheesecloth, unless otherwise directed. Some pickles are crunchy and crisp to the taste, while others are firm but have lost their crispness through cooking.

For all crisp pickles, I recommend the use of kosher salt and white distilled vinegar. Slightly under-ripe vegetables or fruits will also be crunchier to the taste.

Pickles are made with the water-bath method, and all recipes include the processing time required.

Some pickles and relishes may be refrigerated for short-term storage. Relishes may be frozen for a period of no longer than 12 months. Vegetable pickles may not be frozen.

RELISHES & PICKLES

Mom's Pepper Relish • Faye's Zucchini Relish • Spiced Cranberry Relish • Fresh Beet Relish • Pennsylvania Corn Relish • Fruit Relish • Summer Relish • Pickled Okra • Sichuan Pickles • Pickled Pepper • Sour Onion Pickle • Vidalia Onion Pickle • Tex-Mex Pickle • Pickled Baby Vegetables

MOM'S PEPPER RELISH

QUANTITY	8 PINT JARS
METHOD & SHELF LIFE	WATER BATH – 1 YEAR REFRIGERATION – 3 MONTHS MAY BE FROZEN

My husband's very favorite relish is this one. He uses it on sandwiches, salads, meats, poultry and he just eats it plain.

9 sweet red bell peppers, preferably organic, stemmed, seeded and sliced
9 sweet green bell peppers, preferably organic, stemmed, seeded and sliced
9 onions, preferably organic, quartered
3 jalapeño or serrano chilies, preferably organic (optional)
Boiling water
4 cups vinegar
2 cups cold water
3 cups sugar
1 teaspoon salt

Finely shred the bell peppers, onions and, if using, the chilies in the bowl of a food processor fitted with the shredding blade. When shredded, transfer to a heatproof bowl and cover with boiling water. Let stand for 5 minutes; then, drain well. Transfer the drained pepper mixture to a heavy saucepan. Add 2 cups of the vinegar along with the cold water and place over medium heat. Bring to a boil. Immediately, remove from the heat. Let stand for 10 minutes; then drain thoroughly. Return the mixture to the saucepan and add the remaining 2 cups of vinegar along with the sugar and salt. Place over medium heat and again bring to a boil. Lower the heat and cook, stirring occasionally for about 30 minutes. When the mixture has thickened, remove from the heat and immediately pour into hot sterilized jars. Cap and process for 15 minutes in a boiling water bath as directed on pages 30-32.

FAYE'S ZUCCHINI RELISH

QUANTITY	8 PINT JARS

METHOD & SHELF LIFE	WATER BATH – 1 YEAR REFRIGERATION – 6 WEEKS MAY BE FROZEN

This is a friend's mother's answer to the bounty of the summer garden. I truly believe that all zucchini recipes have been developed because of the plant's ability to grow and grow and grow. In the summer, there seems to appear a zucchini fairy who leaves at my back door two or three unasked-for bushels of zucchini. Unasked-for zucchini also seems to appear at the doors of friends, so I know that this mischievous fairy exists! This relish is so tasty you will wish it would multiply on your shelf. It may be used on sandwiches, cold meats and fish or in salads.

NOTE: It is quite simple to grate all of the vegetables in a food processor fitted with the shredding blade.

6 cups grated zucchini, preferably organic
3 cups grated yellow onions, preferably organic
1 sweet red bell pepper, preferably organic, stemmed, seeded and grated
1 sweet green bell pepper, preferably organic, stemmed, seeded and grated
3 tablespoons coarse salt
3 cups sugar
1¼ cups white vinegar
1 teaspoon celery seed
½ teaspoon dry mustard powder
½ teaspoon ground nutmeg
½ teaspoon ground turmeric
½ teaspoon fresh ground black pepper

Place the grated vegetables in a nonreactive bowl. Sprinkle with the salt and toss well to combine. Cover and let stand for 12 hours. Place the mixture in a colander and rinse well under cold running water. Drain thoroughly. Place the sugar, vinegar, celery seed, mustard, nutmeg, turmeric and pepper in a heavy saucepan over medium heat. Bring to a boil; then lower the heat and cook for about 15 minutes, or until mixture begins to thicken. Immediately add vegetable mixture and cook for 30 minutes. Remove from the heat. Pour into hot sterilized jars. Cap and process for 15 minutes in a boiling water bath as directed on pages 30-32.

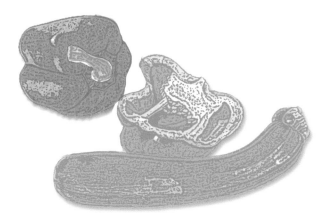

SPICED CRANBERRY RELISH

QUANTITY   FOUR ½-PINT JARS

METHOD   WATER BATH – 1 YEAR
&   REFRIGERATION – 6 WEEKS
SHELF LIFE   MAY BE FROZEN

This is a variation on the traditional Thanksgiving cranberry relish. Don't wait until the holidays to use it as it is wonderfully delicious as an accompaniment to roasted poultry and wild game as well as with patés and terrines.

4½ cups fresh cranberries, preferably organic
¼ cup grated fresh orange zest, preferably organic
¼ cup grated fresh lemon zest, preferably organic
1 tablespoon minced fresh jalapeño chili, preferably organic
1 tablespoon mustard seed
¼ teaspoon dried red pepper flakes
¼ teaspoon ground ginger
1 cup honey
⅔ cup red wine vinegar
Salt to taste

Combine the cranberries, citrus zest, chili, mustard seed, red pepper flakes and ginger in a heavy saucepan. Stir in the honey and vinegar and place over medium heat. Bring to a boil. Lower the heat and simmer for 15 minutes or until slightly thick. Remove from the heat and immediately pour into hot sterilized jars. Cap and process for 10 minutes in a boiling water bath as directed on pages 30-32.

FRESH BEET RELISH

QUANTITY	FOUR ½-PINT JARS
METHOD & SHELF LIFE	WATER BATH — 1 YEAR REFRIGERATION — 6 WEEKS

This is a perfect mate for boiled dinners, or stews or a beautiful garnish to fish and other seafood. It is also a superb base for salad dressings.

NOTE: It is quite simple to grate all of the vegetables in a food processor fitted with the shredding blade.

6 cups peeled and shredded raw beets, preferably organic
1 cup grated fresh horseradish, preferably organic
1 cup grated red onions, preferably organic
1 cup grated zucchini, preferably organic
2 cups distilled white vinegar
1½ cups sugar
1 teaspoon dried red pepper flakes (optional)

Combine the beets, horseradish, onions and zucchini in a heavy saucepan. Stir in the vinegar, sugar and, if using, the red pepper flakes. Place over medium heat and bring to a boil. Lower the heat and simmer for 20 minutes. Remove from the heat and immediately pour into hot sterilized jars. Cap and process for 10 minutes in a boiling water bath as directed on pages 30-32.

PENNSYLVANIA CORN RELISH

QUANTITY   EIGHT ½-PINT JARS

METHOD   WATER BATH – 1 YEAR
&   REFRIGERATION – 8 WEEKS
SHELF LIFE

For generations of Amish, corn relish was always on the table. This relish is almost never seen outside rural communities these days, perhaps because it seems so old fashioned and difficult to make. I have found, however, that it has a wonderful, contemporary taste to which almost everyone favorably responds. Although corn relish is generally used as a condiment or accompaniment to meats or poultry, I combine a jar with 4 cups cold rice or pasta, add a little homemade mayonnaise and have a lovely summer salad. Add some cold leftover meat or poultry, and you have a nice main course meal.

6 cups fresh corn kernels, preferably organic
2 cups finely shredded green cabbage, preferably
    organic
2 cups chopped yellow onions, preferably organic
1 cup seeded and diced red bell pepper, preferably
    organic
2 teaspoons whole celery seed
1 teaspoon whole mustard seed
1 teaspoon ground turmeric
1 teaspoon dry mustard powder
1 cup apple cider vinegar
¾ cup sugar

Combine the corn, cabbage, onions, bell pepper, mustard seed, celery seed, turmeric and dry mustard in a heavy saucepan. Stir in the vinegar and sugar and place over medium heat. Bring to a boil. Lower the heat and simmer gently for 20 minutes. Remove from the heat. Immediately pour into hot sterilized jars. Cap and process for 10 minutes in a boiling water bath as directed on pages 30–32.

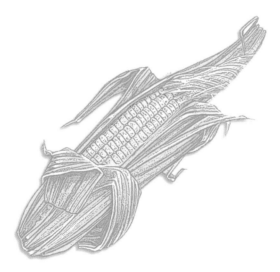

FRUIT RELISH

QUANTITY   SIX ½-PINT JARS

METHOD   WATER BATH – 1 YEAR
   &   REFRIGERATION – 6 WEEKS
SHELF LIFE MAY BE FROZEN

This is a great relish to make in August when peaches, pears and tomatoes are ready for harvest. It is terrific on grilled meats or poultry, or as a condiment with omelettes or other egg-based brunch dishes.

NOTE: It is quite simple to grate or shred all of the vegetables in a food processor fitted with the shredding blade.

2 cups peeled and chopped ripe tomatoes,
    preferably organic
2 cups peeled and shredded pears, preferably organic
2 cups peeled and chopped peaches, preferably organic
1 cup seeded and grated red bell peppers,
    preferably organic
1 cup grated onions, preferably organic
¼ cup peeled and grated fresh ginger, preferably organic
1 teaspoon celery seed
1 teaspoon dry mustard powder
1 teaspoon ground cinnamon
2 cups light brown sugar
1½ cups cider vinegar
½ cup fruit brandy

Combine the tomatoes, pears, peaches, bell peppers, onions, ginger, celery seed, mustard powder and cinnamon in a heavy saucepan. Stir in the sugar, vinegar and fruit brandy and place over medium heat. Bring to a boil; then lower the heat and simmer for 1 hour, stirring frequently to prevent scorching. Remove from the heat. Immediately pour into hot sterilized jars. Cap and process for 15 minutes in a boiling water bath as directed on pages 30–32.

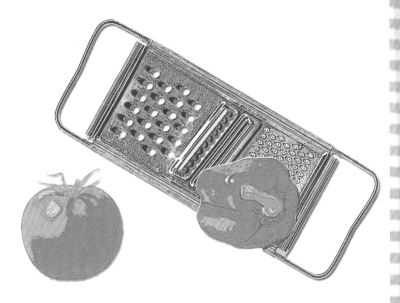

SUMMER RELISH

QUANTITY   SIX ½-PINT JARS

METHOD   NO PROCESSING REQUIRED
&   REFRIGERATION – 1 MONTH
SHELF LIFE

This delightful relish needs no cooking, so it is a perfect preserve to do on a hot summer day when vegetables are at their best. It's a marvelous accompaniment to grilled meats or it can also be used for salad dressings.

3 cups peeled and chopped ripe tomatoes,
    preferably organic
1 cup peeled and chopped green (unripe) tomatoes,
    preferably organic
1 cup chopped onions, preferably organic
1 cup finely shredded cabbage, preferably organic
1 sweet green bell pepper, preferably organic, stemmed,
    seeded and chopped
½ cup peeled and grated sweet apple, preferably organic
2 tablespoons mustard seed
2 teaspoons prepared grated horseradish, preferably organic
1½ cups cider vinegar
⅓ cup light brown sugar
1 teaspoon hot pepper sauce

Combine the tomatoes, onions, cabbage, bell pepper, apple, mustard seed and horseradish in a nonreactive container, such as a large glass bowl. Add the vinegar, sugar and hot pepper sauce, stirring to blend well. Cover and refrigerate for 24 hours before using. If relish gets too juicy, drain off some of the liquid. Cover and refrigerate for up to 1 month.

PICKLED OKRA

QUANTITY   SIX ½-PINT JARS

METHOD   WATER BATH – 1 YEAR
&   REFRIGERATION – 3 MONTHS
SHELF LIFE

*In the 1980s, the interest in Cajun cooking led to the
nationwide discovery of okra, a vegetable most frequently
associated with the South. It is now commonly found in the
produce section of supermarkets. However, I find it best straight
from the garden, small, tender and fragrant. Made into pickle,
it is crisp and delicious, and makes a particularly wonderful hors
d'oeuvre.*

2 cups cider vinegar
1 cup cold water
1¼ cup coarse salt
60 (about 4 pounds) young, tender okra pods,
    preferably organic
6 cloves garlic, preferably organic, peeled
6 jalapeño or serrano chilies, preferably organic
2 tablespoons dill seed
2 tablespoons mustard seed

Combine the vinegar and cold water with the salt in a
heavy saucepan over medium heat. Bring to a boil and
boil for 5 minutes. In the meantime, pack each sterilized
jar with about 10 okra pods, 1 garlic clove, 1 chili and 1
teaspoon each of dill and mustard seed. Pour the boiling
vinegar liquid into each jar, leaving ½-inch headspace.
Cap and process for 15 minutes in a boiling water bath as
directed on pages 30-32.

SICHUAN PICKLES

QUANTITY	SIX ½-PINT JARS

METHOD & SHELF LIFE	WATER BATH – 1 YEAR REFRIGERATION – 6 WEEKS

Almost every town in America seems to have a Chinese restaurant, and every gourmet kitchen has a wok. This pickle is a great accompaniment to not only Sichuan cuisine but to any Chinese or Southeast Asian dish. Frankly, it will add zest to almost any bland dish.

¾ cup red wine vinegar
¾ cup light brown sugar
3 tablespoons soy sauce
8 large seedless cucumbers, preferably organic,
  peeled, seeded and thinly sliced
¼ cup coarse salt
½ cup peanut oil
2 tablespoons Sichuan peppercorns
6 whole dried red chilies
½ cup shredded and soaked Chinese mushrooms
¼ cup grated fresh ginger
1 tablespoon dried red pepper flakes
1 teaspoon minced garlic, preferably organic

Mix vinegar and sugar with the soy sauce in a glass bowl. Cover and set aside for at least 1 hour or up to 24 hours. Place the cucumbers in another glass bowl. Stir in the salt, cover and let stand for 1 hour. Pour oil and peppercorns into wok. Place over high heat and heat to smoking. Lower the heat and cook, stirring until the peppercorns are deeply black and very fragrant. Remove from the heat. Cover and let stand for 20 minutes. Remove the peppercorns from the wok and add the reserved vinegar mixture along with the chilies, mushrooms, ginger, red pepper flakes and garlic. Bring to a boil, stirring frequently. Drain the cucumbers, squeezing out as much liquid as possible. Stir the well-drained cucumbers into boiling liquid. Immediately remove from the heat and pack into hot sterilized jars, leaving ½-inch headspace. Cap and process for 10 minutes in a boiling water bath as directed on pages 30-32.

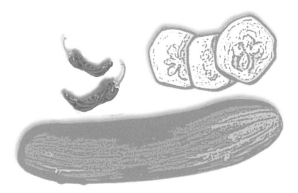

PICKLED PEPPER

QUANTITY   SIX PINT JARS

METHOD   WATER BATH – 1 YEAR
  &   REFRIGERATION – 3 MONTHS
SHELF LIFE

This sensational pickle is as sophisticated as one can imagine yet it comes from the North Union Shaker settlement of the mid-1800s. It was always in great demand by the outside world and is still addictive. Pickled Pepper can be used as an appetizer as well as a garnish or accompaniment.

18 small to medium whole green and/or red bell peppers,
  preferably organic (You may also use very small green
  tomatoes or a mixture of peppers and green tomatoes.)
1 cup coarse salt plus more to taste
1 small head green cabbage, preferably organic,
  finely shredded
3 cups finely shredded onions, preferably organic
1 cup grated fresh horseradish, preferably organic
⅓ cup mustard seed
1 tablespoon ground cloves or to taste
1 teaspoon ground white pepper
1 quart distilled white vinegar
2 cups water
½ cup sugar

Neatly cut tops off of the bell peppers. Carefully remove the seeds, taking care not to break the peppers. Place the seeded peppers along with their tops in large glass or ceramic bowl. Add the salt and cold water to cover by at least an inch. Cover the bowl and set aside for 24 hours. Drain the peppers and tops in a colander and then rinse well under cold running water until completely free of brine. Drain and pat dry. Set aside. Combine the cabbage, onions, horseradish, mustard seed, cloves and pepper in a nonreactive container. Combine the vinegar and water with the sugar in heavy saucepan over medium heat. Bring to a boil; then lower the heat and cook at a bare simmer while you stuff the peppers. While the syrup is simmering, place an equal amount of the cabbage mixture into each pepper. Replace the top on each pepper, holding the top in place with toothpicks or (like the Shakers) sew the top and bottom together using a needle and heavy thread. Pack the stuffed peppers into hot sterilized jars, about 3 per jar. Pour the hot pickling syrup over the peppers, leaving ¼-inch headspace. Cap and process for 15 minutes in a boiling water bath as directed on pages 30-32.

SOUR ONION PICKLE

QUANTITY	FOUR ½-PINT JARS
METHOD & SHELF LIFE	WATER BATH – 1 YEAR REFRIGERATION – 2 MONTHS

This is perfect as a pop-in-your-mouth cocktail tidbit — and also wonderful in salads and sandwiches or as a garnish for cold meats.

4 cups pearl onions, preferably organic (the very
  smallest you can find)
¼ cup coarse salt
3 cups white vinegar
3 tablespoons fresh orange juice
4 dried red hot chilies
¼ cup sugar
1 tablespoon mustard seed
1 tablespoon grated fresh horseradish

Place the peeled onions in glass or ceramic bowl. Sprinkle in the salt and add cold water to cover. Let stand in a cool place for 12 hours. Drain off salt water and rinse the onions in a colander under cold running water. Drain and pat dry. Combine the vinegar and orange juice in a heavy saucepan. Stir in the chilies, sugar, mustard seed and horseradish and place over medium heat. Bring to a boil; then lower the heat and simmer for 15 minutes. Just before the syrup is ready, pack the onions into hot sterilized jars. Pour the hot pickling syrup over onions, leaving ¼-inch headspace. Make sure that each jar contains a chili. Cap and process for 10 minutes in a boiling water bath as directed on pages 30-32.

VIDALIA ONION PICKLE

QUANTITY   SIX PINT JARS

METHOD   WATER BATH – 1 YEAR
&   REFRIGERATION – 6 WEEKS
SHELF LIFE

Vidalia onions are renowned for their sweetness. Developed near Vidalia, Georgia in the 1930s, these native American onions make a superb pickle to be used chopped in a sandwich filling or as a condiment, relish or hors d'oeuvre on a water biscuit with cream cheese.

6 pounds Vidalia onions, preferably organic, quartered
¼ cup salt
Ice chips
5 cups sugar
5 cups distilled white vinegar
2 teaspoons celery seed
2 teaspoons ground turmeric
1 teaspoon dry mustard powder

Layer onions, salt and ice chips in 3 layers in a nonreactive container. Cover and let stand for 3 hours. Drain the onions in a colander. Do not rinse. Using paper towel, squeeze the onions to absorb excess liquid. Set aside. Combine the sugar and vinegar in a heavy saucepan. Stir in the celery seed, turmeric and mustard powder and place over medium heat. Bring to a rolling boil. Add the reserved onions and again bring to a boil. Boil for 3 minutes. Pour into hot sterilized jars, leaving ½-inch headspace. Cap and process for 10 minutes in a boiling water bath as directed on pages 30-32.

TEX-MEX PICKLE

QUANTITY   SIX ½-PINT JARS

METHOD   WATER BATH – 1 YEAR
&   REFRIGERATION – 6 WEEKS
SHELF LIFE

You can use this as a salad mixed with lettuce, as a garnish for any filled tortilla entree or just as a fresh spicy pickle.

2 large jicama, preferably organic, peeled and sliced
   into thin strips
1 large red bell pepper, preferably organic, stemmed,
   seeded and cut into strips
1 large sweet onion, preferably organic, peeled and sliced
1 cup sliced and seeded Anaheim chilies, preferably organic
1 cup radishes, preferably organic, cut into quarters
½ cup chopped scallions, preferably organic
¼ cup coarse salt
3 cups white vinegar
½ cup fresh lime juice
½ cup cold water
2 cups sugar
¼ cup chopped fresh cilantro

Combine jicama, bell pepper, onion, chilies, radishes and scallions in a nonreactive container. Add the salt and coat well. Set aside for 1 hour. Transfer to a colander and rinse thoroughly under cold, running water. Drain well and pat and dry. Combine the vinegar, lime juice and water in a heavy saucepan. Stir in the sugar and cilantro and place over medium heat. Bring to a boil; then, lower the heat and cook for 10 minutes. While the syrup is boiling, pack the vegetables into hot sterilized jars. Pour the boiling pickling syrup over the vegetables in each jar, leaving ¼-inch headspace. Cap and process for 10 minutes in a boiling water bath as directed on pages 30-32.

PICKLED BABY VEGETABLES

QUANTITY   FOUR ½-PINT JARS

METHOD   WATER BATH – 1 YEAR
&   REFRIGERATION – 2 MONTHS
SHELF LIFE

These are especially appealing as a cocktail tidbit or in a salade composé, the classic French composed vegetable salad. Although this recipe calls for baby vegetables, you can also make this pickle with uniform pieces or sticks of any mature vegetable.

3 pounds mixed baby vegetables (for instance, carrots, green
  beans, corn, sugar snap peas, eggplant or pattypan squash)
1 teaspoon salt
2 cups white wine vinegar
4 dried red hot chilies
4 sprigs fresh dill
4 cloves garlic, peeled
1 cinnamon stick
1 tablespoon pickling spice
1 tablespoon cracked black pepper

Place the vegetables in heavy saucepan. Add the salt along with water to cover by at least 1 inch. Place over medium-high heat and bring to a boil. Remove from the heat, cover and let stand for 5 minutes. (If using sugar snap peas, remove them as soon as the water comes to a boil and refresh under cold, running water.) Drain well, reserving 2 cups cooking liquid. Set the vegetables aside. Return the 2 cups of cooking liquid to a heavy saucepan. Add the vinegar, chilies, dill, garlic, cinnamon stick, pickling spice and pepper and place over medium heat. Bring to a boil and boil hard for 10 minutes. Remove from the heat and remove and discard the cinnamon stick. Pack the vegetables along with the syrup into hot sterilized jars, leaving ½-inch headspace. Take care that each jar contains 1 chili, 1 sprig of dill and 1 garlic clove. Cap and process for 15 minutes in a boiling water bath as directed on pages 30-32.

Condiments are made of finely chopped and cooked vegetables and/or fruits. The foods used in preparing many condiments are cooked until tender and then puréed. Usually cooked with vinegars and highly seasoned with spices and peppers, condiments are thick, sauce-like liquids served as sandwich dressing or as seasoning for meats, fish, poultry, game and, occasionally, vegetables.

Salad dressings are made of a combination of oils, vinegars and seasonings. Eggs, creams and cheeses add variety to dressings that are used with vegetable, green or pasta salads while fruit juices, sweeteners and creams complement the basic ingredients for use on fruits.

Most condiments and salad dressings are preserved by cooking in a 10-minute boiling water bath as directed on pages 30–32.

Both may be refrigerated for up to 6 weeks and frozen for a period of no more than 12 months or as directed in the individual recipe.

CONDIMENTS

Spicy Beer Mustard • Bahamian Old Sour • Salsa Inferno •
Nouvelle Catsup • Blueberry Catsup • Condensed Onions • Red
Pepper Mustard • Fresh Horseradish • Mushroom Catsup • Basic
Tex-Mex Salsa

SALAD DRESSINGS

Hot and Sour Salad Dressing • Jalapeño Dressing • Vegetarian
Dressing • Fruit Salad Dressing

SPICY BEER MUSTARD

QUANTITY   FOUR ½-PINT JARS

METHOD   WATER BATH – 1 YEAR
&   REFRIGERATION – 3 MONTHS
SHELF LIFE MAY BE FROZEN

You can use this whenever you might use mustard. It's just better! It particularly makes a terrific coating on grilled or roasted meats or poultry.

1 cup whole mustard seed
1 cup fine quality beer or ale
¼ cup white wine vinegar
3 cups dry English mustard powder
¾ cup light brown sugar
1 teaspoon hot pepper sauce
Coarse salt to taste

Combine mustard seed, beer and vinegar in a nonreactive container. Cover and let stand for 4 hours. Transfer the mustard seed mixture to a heavy saucepan. Stir in the mustard powder, brown sugar and hot pepper sauce. Season with salt to taste and place over low heat. Cook, stirring constantly for 10 minutes. Add additional beer, a drop or two at a time, if mixture seems too dry. It should be the consistency of Dijon mustard. Pour into hot sterilized jars. Cap and process for 15 minutes in a boiling water bath as directed on pages 30-32.

BAHAMIAN OLD SOUR

QUANTITY	FOUR ½-PINT JARS
METHOD & SHELF LIFE	NO PROCESSING REQUIRED, TIGHTLY SEALED IN COOL SPOT FOR UP TO 1 YEAR REFRIGERATION – 2 MONTHS

We were introduced to this as a seasoning on conch served on Harbour Island in the Bahamas. Every cook has a jar or two on the shelf and every island roadside food stand has its own homemade Old Sour. We have become addicted to it. It is perfect for sprinkling on fish either before or after cooking, and on vegetables and salads.

4 cups fresh Key lime, lime, lemon or sour orange juice
2 tablespoons salt
16 Scotch bonnet, Thai bird, jalapeño or any other
 hot chili

Combine the juice and salt in a nonreactive container, stirring until the salt is dissolved. Pour into hot sterilized jars. Add 4 peppers to each jar. Screw clean caps on tightly and store for at least 10 days before use.

SALSA INFERNO

QUANTITY	THREE ½-PINT JARS

METHOD & SHELF LIFE	WATER BATH – 1 YEAR REFRIGERATION – 1 MONTH MAY BE FROZEN

This is the hottest sauce I know for garnishing Tex-Mex foods — tacos, burritos and the like. It can also be used on grilled meats and vegetables but remember: it is hot!

4 cups peeled and chopped fresh tomatoes,
  preferably organic
1 cup chopped mild green chilies, preferably organic
½ cup chopped scallions, preferably organic
½ cup stemmed, seeded and chopped jalapeño chilies,
  preferably organic
½ cup minced red onions, preferably organic
2 tablespoons minced garlic, preferably organic
1 tablespoon hot pepper sauce
3 tablespoons distilled white vinegar
Salt, optional

Combine the tomatoes, green chilies, scallions, jalapeños, onions and garlic in a heavy saucepan. Stir in the vinegar and hot pepper sauce. Place over medium heat and, if using, season with salt. Bring to a boil. Immediately remove from the heat and pack into hot sterilized jars. Cap and process for 10 minutes in a boiling water bath as directed on pages 30-32.

NOUVELLE CATSUP

QUANTITY FOUR ½-PINT JARS

METHOD WATER BATH – 1 YEAR
& REFRIGERATION – 1 WEEK
SHELF LIFE MAY BE FROZEN

This is not really a classic catsup, but similar in consistency and piquancy. It is used as a sauce of accompaniment to game (venison, in particular) or meat, especially pork. Using no salt, no oil and no cream, this catsup is most useful to people with health or diet issues.

4 cups trimmed, peeled and sliced turnips,
 preferably organic
3 cups peeled, cored and chopped tart apples,
 preferably organic
1 cup trimmed, peeled and sliced parsnips,
 preferably organic
1 cup trimmed, peeled, cored and sliced hard pear,
 preferably organic
½ cup chopped celery, preferably organic
One 4-inch piece lemon peel, preferably organic
One 1-inch piece fresh ginger, preferably organic,
 peeled and cut into quarters
1 tablespoon fresh lemon juice, preferably organic
½ teaspoon hot pepper sauce
Salt and pepper to taste, optional

Combine the turnips, apples, parsnips, pear and celery on a steamer rack in a large heavy saucepan. Lay the lemon peel and ginger pieces on top. Pour enough water into the bottom of the pan to keep an active steam going to cook the vegetables and fruits. This is the best method to hold the individual flavor of each component. (If you do not have a steamer, cook the vegetables or fruits in a heavy saucepan with just enough water to keep them from sticking as they steam.) Place over medium-high heat and steam for about 15 minutes or just until the vegetables and fruits are soft. If the water is evaporating too quickly, lower the heat. If necessary, add additional hot water.

Remove from the heat and discard the lemon peel and ginger. Drain the vegetables and fruits in a fine mesh sieve, reserving the steaming liquid. Transfer the vegetable and fruit mixture to the bowl of a food processor fitted with the metal blade. This may have to be done in batches. Process until puréed. If necessary, add the reserved steaming liquid, a bit at a time, to achieve a smooth purée.

Transfer the purée to a heavy, nonreactive saucepan. Stir in the lemon juice and hot pepper sauce and season with salt and pepper to taste. Place over medium heat and bring to a simmer. Cook at a gentle simmer for 5 minutes. Remove from the heat and immediately pour into hot sterilized jars, leaving ½-inch headspace. Cap and process for 20 minutes in a boiling water bath as directed on pages 30-32.

BLUEBERRY CATSUP

QUANTITY   FOUR ½-PINT JARS

METHOD   WATER BATH — 1 YEAR
&   REFRIGERATION — 3 MONTHS
SHELF LIFE MAY BE FROZEN

This is another hand-me-down from the North Union Shaker settlement, and one of my favorite condiments to make a culinary statement with simple foods.

5 cups fresh blueberries, preferably organic
3 cups sugar
1 tablespoon fresh lemon juice
1 tablespoon ground cinnamon
2 teaspoons ground cloves
1 teaspoon fresh ground black pepper
½ teaspoon salt (or to taste)
¾ cup blueberry vinegar

Combine the blueberries and sugar in a heavy saucepan. Stir in the lemon juice, cinnamon, cloves, pepper and salt. Add the vinegar and place over medium heat. Bring to a boil; then, lower the heat and simmer, stirring frequently, until berries have disintegrated and the catsup is thick.
Remove from the heat and immediately pour into hot sterilized jars. Cap and process for 15 minutes in a boiling water bath as directed on pages 30-32.

CONDENSED ONIONS

QUANTITY   THREE ½-PINT JARS

METHOD   WATER BATH – 1 YEAR
&   REFRIGERATION – 2 MONTHS
SHELF LIFE   MAY BE FROZEN

This is a very special condiment for grilled pork, chicken or game. Just remember that the sweeter the onion (Vidalia or Walla-Walla onions are best), the richer the finished preserve.

¾ cup sweet butter
2 tablespoons virgin olive oil
8 cups peeled, halved and sliced sweet onions,
    preferably organic
2 cloves garlic, preferably organic, peeled and minced
½ cup superfine sugar
½ cup fruit vinegar
1 teaspoon minced fresh thyme

Combine the butter with the oil in heavy saucepan over medium heat. When hot, stir in the onions and garlic and cook for 10 minutes. Add the sugar, vinegar and thyme. Cook, stirring constantly, until sugar is dissolved and mixture begins to turn caramel colored. Lower the heat and cook, stirring frequently, for about 15 minutes or until thick and very dark caramel in color. If, during cooking, more liquid is needed to keep onions from scorching, add additional fruit vinegar. When the mixture is thick, pour into hot sterilized jars. Cap and process for 15 minutes in a boiling water bath as directed on pages 30-32.

RED PEPPER MUSTARD

QUANTITY   FOUR ½-PINT JARS

METHOD   WATER BATH — 1 YEAR
&   REFRIGERATION — 3 MONTHS
SHELF LIFE   MAY BE FROZEN

A perfect mustard for all types of sandwiches, as well as a special coating when roasting pork or lamb. Mix this mustard with whipped cream or cook a bit with heavy cream and you will have an easy "haute cuisine" sauce.

1 cup fine dry English mustard powder
¼ cup light brown sugar
1 cup fruit vinegar, such as raspberry
1 cup water
½ teaspoon hot pepper sauce
4 cups roasted red bell pepper purée, preferably organic
½ cup dry sherry
¼ cup mustard seed
¼ teaspoon ground oregano
¾ cup chopped, cooked mixed red and green bell peppers, preferably organic

Combine the mustard powder with the sugar in a nonreactive container. Stir in the vinegar, water and hot pepper sauce. Cover and let stand for 3 hours. Combine bell pepper purée with sherry, mustard seed and oregano in a heavy saucepan. Place over medium heat and bring to a boil. Immediately stir in the reserved mustard powder mixture and again bring to a boil. Lower the heat and cook, stirring constantly until mixture is fairly thick. Quickly stir in cooked, red and green bell pepper pieces and immediately pour into hot sterilized jars. Cap and process for 15 minutes in a boiling water bath as directed on pages 30-32.

FRESH HORSERADISH

QUANTITY   SIX ½-PINT JARS

METHOD   NO PROCESSING REQUIRED
&   REFRIGERATION — UP TO 6 MONTHS
SHELF LIFE

I first discovered the ease of preparation and fresh taste of home-canned horseradish in the Pennsylvania Amish country. I use it so frequently in sauces, salads, on sandwiches and, particularly, as a low-calorie and quite zesty relish that I always try to have it on hand.

3 pounds fresh horseradish, preferably organic,
  peeled and finely grated
1 raw red beet, preferably organic, finely grated,
  optional for red color and a hint of sweetness
1½ cups excellent white vinegar or white herb vinegar

Pack the grated horseradish (and beet, if using) into hot sterilized jars. Fill each jar to the top with vinegar. Cover with a clean, tight seal and refrigerate.

Refrigerate for 1 week before using.

BASIC TEX-MEX SALSA

QUANTITY	FOUR ½-PINT JARS
METHOD & SHELF LIFE	WATER BATH – 1 YEAR REFRIGERATION – 1 WEEK MAY BE FROZEN – IF FREEZING FIRST, DO NOT COOK

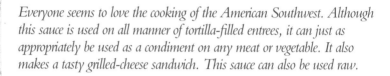

Everyone seems to love the cooking of the American Southwest. Although this sauce is used on all manner of tortilla-filled entrees, it can just as appropriately be used as a condiment on any meat or vegetable. It also makes a tasty grilled-cheese sandwich. This sauce can also be used raw.

1 jalapeño chili, preferably organic, stemmed,
  seeded and minced
4 cups cored, peeled, seeded and chopped ripe
  tomatoes, preferably organic
1 cup finely chopped red onions, preferably organic
½ cup seeded and chopped mild green chilies [See NOTE.]
1 teaspoon chopped garlic, preferably organic
¼ cup chopped fresh cilantro, preferably organic
¼ cup red wine vinegar
2 tablespoons olive oil
Salt to taste

NOTE: You can, if desired, use a food processor to chop the vegetables and/or herbs but if you do, take care not to purée them. This sauce should have a nice chunky texture.

For a cooked sauce, combine all ingredients in heavy saucepan. Place over medium heat and bring to a boil. Stir in the cilantro, vinegar and olive oil, season with salt to taste and return to the boil. Immediately remove from the heat and pour into hot sterilized jars. Cap and process for 15 minutes in a boiling water bath as directed on pages 30-32.

If using as a fresh salsa or freezing, mix all of the ingredients together in a nonreactive container, cover and let stand for about 30 minutes before using or freezing.

MUSHROOM CATSUP

QUANTITY	FOUR ½-PINT JARS
METHOD & SHELF LIFE	WATER BATH – 1 YEAR REFRIGERATION – 1 WEEK MAY BE FROZEN

This is an interesting variation on one of America's most used condiments. Not at all new, this long-forgotten recipe is a perfect garnish for all grilled meats and poultry.

8 cups chopped fresh mushrooms
1 tablespoon salt
1 jalapeño chili preferably organic, seeded and chopped,
  optional
1 cup chopped onions, preferably organic
1 teaspoon minced garlic, preferably organic
1 teaspoon commercial pickling spices
1 tablespoon chopped fresh parsley
½ cup herb vinegar

Combine the chopped mushrooms with the salt in a glass bowl, stirring to blend. Cover and set aside for 24 hours. Combine the salted mushrooms with the chili, if using, and the onions, garlic, pickling spices and parsley in a heavy saucepan. Stir in the vinegar and place over medium heat. Bring to a boil. Lower the heat and simmer for 45 minutes or until thick. Remove from the heat and drain through a fine mesh sieve, separately reserving all of the liquid. Transfer the mushroom mixture to the bowl of a food processor fitted with the metal blade, adding reserved liquid as needed to make a thick catsup-like sauce. Transfer the purée to a heavy saucepan over medium heat and bring to a boil. Immediately pour into hot sterilized jars. Cap and process for 20 minutes in a boiling water bath as directed on pages 30-32.

HOT AND SOUR SALAD DRESSING

QUANTITY	THREE ½-PINT JARS
METHOD & SHELF LIFE	WATER BATH — 1 YEAR REFRIGERATION — 1 WEEK MAY BE FROZEN

This Chinese-inspired salad dressing is perfect for use to season pasta, poultry and vegetable or mixed green salads.

2½ cups vegetable stock
½ cup fruit vinegar
¼ cup peanut oil
¼ cup soy sauce
¼ cup dry white wine
2 tablespoons hot chili oil [See NOTE.]
⅓ cup crunchy peanut butter
2 tablespoons sesame seeds
2 tablespoons grated fresh ginger
2 teaspoons garlic, peeled and minced
2 teaspoons dried red pepper flakes (or to taste)

NOTE: Hot chili oil is available from Asian markets, specialty food stores and many supermarkets.

Combine the vegetable stock, vinegar, peanut oil, soy sauce, white wine and chili oil in the bowl of a food processor fitted with the metal blade. Using quick on-and-off turns, thoroughly combine. Add the peanut butter, sesame seeds, ginger, garlic and red pepper flakes and process until well blended. Transfer the dressing to a heavy saucepan over medium heat. Cook until just hot. Immediately pour into hot sterilized jars. Cap and process for 12 minutes in a boiling water bath as directed on pages 30-32.

JALAPEÑO DRESSING

QUANTITY   TWO ½-PINT JARS

METHOD   WATER BATH – 1 YEAR
&   REFRIGERATION – 2 WEEKS
SHELF LIFE MAY BE FROZEN

*This zesty dressing for vegetables or cold meats also makes an
interesting addition to sandwich fillings such as tuna or egg salad.*

6 cloves garlic, preferably organic peeled
3 fresh jalapeño chilies, preferably organic,
  stemmed, seeded and chopped
½ cup chopped cilantro, preferably organic
¼ cup chopped parsley, preferably organic
¼ cup chopped scallions, preferably organic
2 cups fruit vinegar
¾ cup safflower oil
½ cup virgin olive oil

Combine the garlic, chilies, cilantro, parsley and scallions in
a blender jar. Add the vinegar along with the safflower and
olive oils. Quickly process until almost smooth. Transfer to
a heavy saucepan over medium heat. Cook until just hot.
Immediately pour into hot sterilized jars. Cap and process for
15 minutes in a boiling water bath as directed on pages 30-32.

VEGETARIAN DRESSING

QUANTITY   FOUR ½-PINT JARS

METHOD   WATER BATH – 1 YEAR
&   REFRIGERATION – 2 WEEKS
SHELF LIFE   MAY BE FROZEN

*Low calorie, healthful and tasty – what more could you want?
This is a great dressing for green or vegetable salads that can also
be used on sandwiches.*

3 cups chopped fresh red tomatoes, preferably organic
1 cup chopped onions, preferably organic
¾ cup chopped celery, preferably organic
¾ cup chopped fresh chives, preferably organic
¾ cup chopped fresh parsley, preferably organic
1 teaspoon chopped garlic, preferably organic
1 teaspoon chopped basil, preferably organic
2 cups water
1 cup herb vinegar [See NOTE.]
1 tablespoon vegetarian seasoning
   (available in health food stores)

NOTE: To make your own herb vinegar ahead of time,
see pages 177-178.

Combine the tomatoes, onions, celery, chives, parsley,
garlic and basil in a heavy saucepan. Stir in the water,
vinegar and seasoning and place over medium heat.
Bring to a boil. Lower the heat and cook for 10 minutes.
Remove from the heat and pour into a blender.
Process to a smooth purée. Return the purée to a clean
saucepan and place over medium heat. Bring to a boil
and immediately remove from the heat. Pour into hot
sterilized jars. Cap and process for 20 minutes in a boiling
water bath as directed on pages 30-32.

FRUIT SALAD DRESSING

QUANTITY	FOUR ½-PINT JARS
METHOD & SHELF LIFE	WATER BATH – 1 YEAR REFRIGERATION – 2 WEEKS MAY BE FROZEN

This mix is the perfect coating for all fruit salads. But, it can also be used in mixed green salads combined with citrus sections or as a dressing for grilled fish or poultry. When using, you can thin the dressing with some yogurt, sour cream or whipped cream for a richer taste.

2 cups fresh raspberry purée, preferably organic
1 teaspoon grated fresh orange zest
1 teaspoon grated fresh lemon zest
1 teaspoon grated fresh ginger
⅛ teaspoon ground curry powder
¼ cup Triple Sec or other orange flavored liqueur

Combine the raspberry purée with the citrus zests, ginger and curry powder in a heavy saucepan. Stir in the liqueur and place over medium heat. Cook until just hot. Remove from the heat and immediately pour into hot sterilized jars. Cap and process for 10 minutes in a boiling water bath as directed on pages 30-32.

Chapter 8

MAIN COURSE SAUCES

Sauces are dressings for vegetables, meats or pasta used when you wish to add flavor and provide richness, color and/or moisture.

They are usually cooked and can be made from either creams, acids, stocks or chopped vegetables with added seasonings.

Chopped vegetable and stock-based sauces are generally used on pastas and meats. Sauces having an acid base are most frequently used as cold or room temperature garnishes for seafood, meat, poultry, game or vegetables.

Main course sauces are my favorite preserves as they can quickly and easily give a delectable unexpected center to a meal. Such sauces are usually preserved by the boiling water bath as described on pages 30-32. Or they may be refrigerated for short-term storage or frozen for a period of no longer than 6 months. Most will require reheating before use.

MAIN COURSE SAUCES

Pesto • My Own Barbeque Sauce • Gazpacho Sauce • Teriyaki Sauce • Mushroom Sauce • Creole Sauce • Tuna Sauce • Homemade Tomato Sauce

PESTO

QUANTITY   FOUR ½-PINT JARS

METHOD   REFRIGERATION – 2 WEEKS
&   MAY BE FROZEN – UP TO 6 MONTHS
SHELF LIFE

Pesto has become a year-round pasta or salad sauce due to the almost continuous availability of fresh basil in the supermarket. However, since basil is so prolific, pesto can usually be made very cheaply during the summer months. You can process in a 15-minute boiling water bath, but I really prefer the fresh taste of the frozen. Pesto is traditionally served as a sauce for linguine or spaghetti, but it is also delicious on fish or poultry.

8 cups coarsely chopped fresh basil, preferably organic,
   packed tightly
1½ cups fine-quality olive oil
2 cups pine nuts [See NOTE.]
2 cloves garlic, peeled and chopped
2 cups freshly grated Parmesan cheese
1 teaspoon fresh ground pepper

NOTE: Pesto can also be made with almonds, hazelnuts or walnuts.

Combine the basil, nuts and garlic in the bowl of food processor fitted with the metal blade. Process to just blend. With the motor running, add the oil and, when blended, add the cheese. This may have to be done in batches. Season with pepper to taste. Pack into hot sterilized jars or sterilized containers and freeze as directed on pages 33-34.

MY OWN BARBEQUE SAUCE

QUANTITY   FOUR PINT JARS

METHOD   WATER BATH – 1 YEAR
&   REFRIGERATION – 2 WEEKS
SHELF LIFE   MAY BE FROZEN

Like almost every grill-master I know, I think that my barbecue sauce IS the best. In fact, I know it is! I use it on meat, fish, poultry and, of course, summer's grilled spareribs. I devised this sauce one summer when I was overwhelmed with tomatoes but you can use canned tomato purée if desired.

10 cups peeled, cored, seeded and chopped very ripe tomatoes, preferably organic
3 cups chopped onions, preferably organic
1 cup seeded and chopped red bell pepper, preferably organic
½ cup peeled and chopped celery, preferably organic
1 cup light brown sugar
1 cup red wine vinegar
¼ cup fresh lemon juice
¼ cup Worcestershire sauce
2 tablespoons dry English mustard powder
2 tablespoons commercial chili powder
1 tablespoon dried red pepper flakes
1 teaspoon hot pepper sauce
1 teaspoon freshly grated lemon zest, preferably organic

Combine the tomatoes, onions, bell pepper and celery in a heavy saucepan. Add just enough water to barely cover and place over medium heat. Bring to a boil; then, lower the heat and simmer for about 20 minutes or until the vegetables are very soft. Remove from the heat and pour into a blender jar. Process to a smooth purée. Transfer the purée to a heavy saucepan. Stir in the brown sugar, vinegar, lemon juice, Worcestershire sauce, mustard powder, chili powder, red pepper flakes, hot pepper sauce and lemon zest.

Place over medium heat and cook, stirring frequently, for about 1 hour, or until the mixture is thick. Remove from the heat and immediately pour into hot sterilized jars, leaving ¼-inch headspace. Cap and process for 20 minutes in a boiling water bath as directed on pages 30-32.

GAZPACHO SAUCE

QUANTITY	SIX ½-PINT JARS
METHOD & SHELF LIFE	WATER BATH – 1 YEAR REFRIGERATION – 2 DAYS MAY BE FROZEN

A perfect covering for cold beef, this sauce can also be used on other meats, fish or poultry. It may be served hot or cold. Gazpacho Sauce may also be used immediately or frozen, uncooked.

2 cucumbers, preferably organic, peeled,
  seeded and chopped fine
4 cups fresh tomato purée, preferably organic
½ cup chopped red bell pepper, preferably organic
½ cup chopped red onion, preferably organic
½ cup peeled and chopped celery, preferably organic
¼ cup grated fresh horseradish, preferably organic
2 tablespoons chopped fresh parsley, preferably organic
1 tablespoon chopped fresh tarragon, preferably organic
½ cup red wine vinegar
Salt and pepper to taste

Combine the cucumbers with the tomato purée, bell pepper, onion, celery, horseradish, parsley and tarragon in a heavy saucepan. Stir in the vinegar and place over medium heat. Bring to a boil. Lower the heat, season with salt and pepper and simmer for 20 minutes, stirring frequently. Remove from the heat. Immediately pour into hot sterilized jars, leaving ½-inch headspace. Cap and process for 15 minutes in a boiling water bath as directed on pages 30-32.

TERIYAKI SAUCE

QUANTITY   FOUR ½-PINT JARS

METHOD   WATER BATH — 1 YEAR
&   REFRIGERATION — 1 MONTH
SHELF LIFE   MAY BE FROZEN

Probably not too close to the Japanese original but truly an American favorite. Great as a marinade for any meat, poultry or fish, and it's equally good thickened a bit with arrowroot when you need a quick gravy.

3 cups safflower oil
1½ cups mild soy sauce
1½ cups unprocessed honey
2 tablespoons rice vinegar
1 tablespoon tomato paste
1 cup chopped scallions
1 tablespoon grated fresh ginger
1 teaspoon minced garlic, preferably organic
Dash hot pepper sauce

Combine the oil with the soy sauce, honey, vinegar and tomato paste in a heavy saucepan, stirring to blend. Add the scallions, ginger, garlic and hot pepper sauce, and place over medium heat. Bring to a boil. Lower the heat and simmer for 15 minutes. Remove from the heat and immediately pour into hot sterilized jars. Cap and process for 15 minutes in a boiling water bath as directed on pages 30-32.

MUSHROOM SAUCE

QUANTITY	THREE PINT JARS

METHOD & SHELF LIFE	WATER BATH – 1 YEAR REFRIGERATION – 1 WEEK MAY BE FROZEN

This has saved me many times, as it can change leftover meats into a superb new meal as quickly as you can open the container. You can prepare this sauce with dried French or Italian mushrooms for a more pungent taste.

½ cup sweet butter, at room temperature
¼ cup olive oil
6 cups sliced fresh mushrooms, preferably organic (or same
   amount of soaked and sliced dried mushrooms)
1 cup grated onions, preferably organic
½ cup grated carrots, preferably organic
¼ cup chopped fresh parsley, preferably organic
1 teaspoon minced garlic, preferably organic
3 cups good dry red wine
1 cup water
1 tablespoon chopped fresh rosemary, preferably organic
¼ cup cornstarch dissolved in ¼ cup red wine,
   vegetable broth or water
Salt and pepper to taste

Combine the butter and olive oil in a heavy saucepan over medium heat. Add mushrooms, onions, carrots, parsley and garlic and sauté until mushrooms begin to lose their water and brown a bit. Remove the vegetables from pan and set aside. Keeping the pan on medium heat, add the wine, water and rosemary. Bring to a boil, stirring constantly, scraping up any bits stuck to the bottom of the pan. Whisk the cornstarch mixture into the boiling red wine mixture, stirring constantly until thickened. Add the reserved vegetables and again bring to a boil. Remove from heat and immediately pour into hot sterilized jars, leaving ½-inch headspace. Cap and process 20 minutes in a boiling-water bath as directed on pages 30-32, or freeze in sterilized containers as directed on pages 33-34.

CREOLE SAUCE

QUANTITY FOUR PINT JARS

METHOD WATER BATH – 1 YEAR
& REFRIGERATION – 1 WEEK
SHELF LIFE MAY BE FROZEN

Cajun (country style), Creole (New Orleans style), call it what you will, Louisiana has given us some wonderful foods. This sauce is great cooked with seafood, ground meats and chicken, and creates a fantastic meal, done with shrimp and dirty rice.

12 cups peeled, cored, seeded and chopped
 very ripe tomatoes, preferably organic
2 cups chopped red onions, preferably organic
1 cup chopped green bell peppers, preferably organic
1 tablespoon minced garlic, preferably organic
2 dried hot red chilies, preferably organic
1 tablespoon minced fresh rosemary, preferably organic
1 teaspoon ground bay leaf
1 teaspoon ground thyme

Combine the tomatoes with the onions, bell pepper and garlic in a heavy saucepan, stirring to blend. Add the chilies, rosemary, bay leaf and thyme and place over medium heat. Bring to a boil. Lower the heat and simmer, stirring frequently for about 1 hour. Remove from the heat and immediately pour into hot sterilized jars, leaving ½-inch headspace. Cap and process for 20 minutes in a boiling water bath as directed on pages 30-32.

TUNA SAUCE

QUANTITY	FOUR ½-PINT JARS
METHOD & SHELF LIFE	REFRIGERATION – 2 HOURS MAY BE FROZEN – UP TO 6 MONTHS

This is one of my favorite main course sauces. It is based on the sauce used in the classic Italian dish, vitello tonnato. *I keep it in the freezer for use on cold salads, poached chicken or veal. It can immediately turn a simple meal into a gourmet dinner.*

12 large egg yolks, preferably from free range chickens
¼ cup red wine vinegar
¼ cup fresh lemon juice
1 teaspoon dry English mustard powder
1 teaspoon capers
1½ cups virgin olive oil
Six 6½-ounce cans tuna packed in olive oil, drained
½ cup drained anchovy fillets
¾ cup fresh dairy sour cream

Combine the egg yolks with the vinegar, lemon juice, mustard powder and capers in the bowl of a food processor fitted with the metal blade. With motor running, add the olive oil followed by the tuna and anchovies. When well blended, add sour cream. Immediately pour into sterilized containers and freeze as directed on pages 33-34.

HOMEMADE TOMATO SAUCE

QUANTITY	SIX PINT JARS

METHOD & SHELF LIFE	WATER BATH – 1 YEAR REFRIGERATION – 3 DAYS MAY BE FROZEN – 6 MONTHS TO 1 YEAR

This is, perhaps, my all-time favorite sauce. I am never without a few containers in the freezer. It can be used as is or as the base for all types of Italian pasta sauces, soups or gravy for roasts or poultry.

¼ cup olive oil
2 tablespoons minced garlic, preferably organic
10 cups peeled, cored, seeded and chopped
  very ripe tomatoes, preferably organic
1 tablespoon sugar
Salt and pepper to taste
2 cups chopped fresh basil, preferably organic

Heat the olive oil in a heavy saucepan over medium heat. Add the garlic and cook, stirring frequently, for about 2 minutes or until fragrant. Stir in the tomatoes and sugar and bring to a simmer. Lower the heat, season with salt and pepper and cook for 20 minutes. Stir in the basil. Pour into sterilized containers and freeze as directed on pages 33-34. Or, pour into hot sterilized jars, leaving ½-inch headspace. Cap and process for 20 minutes in a boiling water bath as directed on pages 30-32.

CHAPTER 9

DESSERT SAUCES & SYRUPS

Dessert or sweet sauces are, for the most part, used as toppings for ice cream, cakes, puddings or fruit. Occasionally a sweet sauce will be used as an accompaniment to, or as a basting for, meats, poultry or game. These sauces may be made from chopped or puréed fruit or from chocolate, citrus or liqueur bases.

Syrups may be used as toppings on breakfast breads (such as pancakes or waffles), with ice cream, as cake glazes or in drinks. The flavor and consistency will most frequently dictate use. They are generally made from fruit purée or juice, spices or liqueurs.

Dessert sauces and syrups can be preserved by the water bath method as described on pages 30-32. All may be refrigerated for short-term storage or frozen for up to a period of no more than 6 months. Some will require reheating before use.

DESSERT SAUCES

White Chocolate Sauce • All-Purpose Berry Sauce • Cranberry Rum Sauce • Sambuca Sauce • Melba Sauce • Praline Sauce • Shaker Lemon Sauce • Killer Chocolate Fudge Sauce

SYRUPS

Basic Sugar Syrup • Spiced Blueberry Syrup • Rum Syrup • Red Hot Apple Syrup

WHITE CHOCOLATE SAUCE

QUANTITY	FOUR ½-PINT JARS
METHOD & SHELF LIFE	REFRIGERATION – 2 WEEKS MAY BE FROZEN – 6 MONTHS

This is unusual in its use of white chocolate but traditional in sweet taste. You can create variety by adding liqueur or toasted, chopped nuts. The result is a perfect topping on homemade ice cream, particularly chocolate.

⅔ cup unsalted butter, at room temperature
18 ounces white chocolate
1 cup heavy cream
1 teaspoon pure vanilla extract
1 cup toasted chopped nut meats or 2 tablespoons
  liqueur of your choice (optional)

Melt butter in top half of a double boiler over very hot water. When melted, stir in chocolate until well blended. Add the cream and vanilla, stirring until thoroughly blended. If using, stir in the nuts or liqueur. Remove from the heat and immediately pour into sterilized containers. Refrigerate or freeze as directed on pages 32-34.

ALL-PURPOSE BERRY SAUCE

QUANTITY	FOUR ½-PINT JARS
METHOD & SHELF LIFE	REFRIGERATION – 3 DAYS MAY BE FROZEN – 6 MONTHS

This sauce can be used as is or expanded upon for dessert sauces, salads or meats. I keep it in my freezer at all times, for use whenever a berry purée is called for.

2 quarts berries (raspberries, strawberries, blueberries,
   etc.), washed and hulled
½ cup water
1 teaspoon fresh lemon juice
Sugar to taste

Place berries in a heavy saucepan over medium heat. Add the water and lemon juice. Cover and cook for about 15 minutes or until the berries are very soft. Remove from the heat and transfer the berries to the bowl of a food processor fitted with the metal blade. Process to a smooth purée. Strain the purée through a fine mesh sieve, discarding the seeds. Return the berry purée to a heavy saucepan. Taste for sweetness; add sugar if necessary (but not more than ¼ cup at a time). Place over medium heat and bring to a boil. Lower the heat and cook for 5 minutes. Remove from the heat and immediately pour into sterilized containers and refrigerate or freeze as directed on pages 32-34.

CRANBERRY-RUM SAUCE

QUANTITY   FOUR ½-PINT JARS

METHOD   WATER BATH – 1 YEAR
&   REFRIGERATION – 2 WEEKS
SHELF LIFE

This is a wonderful sauce served over ice cream or on baked puddings or pound cake. It can also be eaten alone with a dollop of sour cream. To serve you may add a little fresh rum and then carefully ignite each serving for a spectacular display.

2 cups sugar
1 cup water
1 cinnamon stick, broken into pieces
4 cups cranberries, preferably organic
1 cup good-quality rum
1 tablespoon cornstarch dissolved in 1 tablespoon
   water or rum

Combine the sugar and water in a heavy saucepan. Add the cinnamon stick and place over medium heat. Bring to a boil. Lower the heat and cook for 10 minutes. Remove the cinnamon stick and add the cranberries and rum. Bring to a simmer and cook for 10 more minutes. Stir the cornstarch mixture into the sauce and cook for an additional 5 minutes. Remove from the heat and immediately pour into hot sterilized jars. Cap and process for 10 minutes in a boiling water bath as directed on pages 30-32.

SAMBUCA SAUCE

QUANTITY	TWO ½-PINT JARS

METHOD & SHELF LIFE	REFRIGERATION – 1 WEEK MAY BE FROZEN – 6 MONTHS

A wonderful dessert topping that should be served warm. I usually make a small jar of coffee beans covered with Sambuca to be used as a garnish with this sauce.

¼ pound bittersweet chocolate
⅔ cup sweet butter
¼ cup cocoa powder
¼ cup instant espresso coffee powder
1 cup light brown sugar
⅓ cup half-and-half
⅓ cup Sambuca Romana or other anise-flavored
  liqueur

Combine the chocolate and butter in the top half of a double boiler over very hot water. Heat, stirring frequently until melted. When well-blended, add the cocoa and coffee, stirring constantly. When blended, add the brown sugar, half-and-half and liqueur. Cook, stirring frequently until the sauce is thick. Remove from the heat and immediately pour into sterilized containers and refrigerate or freeze as directed on pages 32-34.

MELBA SAUCE

QUANTITY	FOUR ½-PINT JARS
METHOD & SHELF LIFE	WATER BATH – 1 YEAR REFRIGERATION – 2 WEEKS

This is great to have on hand! It is used in the classic Peaches Melba, a dessert comprised of vanilla ice cream, peaches and raspberry sauce, named for Dame Nellie Melba, the Australian opera singer who wowed Europe in the late 19th century. Vanilla ice cream and fresh fruit topped with Melba Sauce is a memorable finish for any meal.

3 cups fresh raspberry purée, preferably organic, strained
1 cup Cassis Jelly (see page 47) or fine-quality
   commercially preserved currant jelly
1 cup superfine sugar
1 tablespoon lemon juice
½ teaspoon grated fresh lemon zest, preferably organic
1 teaspoon cornstarch dissolved in 1 tablespoon cold water

Combine the raspberry purée with the jelly and sugar in a heavy saucepan over medium heat. Bring to a boil and add the lemon juice and zest. Then stir in the cornstarch mixture. Cook, stirring frequently for about 15 minutes or until sauce is clear and thick. Immediately pour into hot sterilized jars. Cap and process for 15 minutes in a boiling water bath as directed on pages 30-32.

PRALINE SAUCE

QUANTITY	FOUR ½-PINT JARS

METHOD & SHELF LIFE	REFRIGERATION– 1 WEEK MAY BE FROZEN – 6 MONTHS

This is a rich, extra special dessert sauce, rather like the filling for a pecan pie. It is so rich that it should be used in moderation.

8 large egg yolks, preferably from free range chickens
1 cup light brown sugar
¼ cup unsalted butter, at room temperature
1 cup heavy cream
3 tablespoons fine quality bourbon
3 cups toasted pecans

Combine the egg yolks with the sugar and butter in a heavy saucepan over low heat. Cook, stirring constantly until thoroughly blended. Stir in the cream and bourbon, raise the heat and bring to a boil. Lower the heat and simmer for about 5 minutes, stirring constantly. Add the pecans. Remove from the heat and immediately pour into sterilized containers and refrigerate or freeze as directed on pages 32–34.

SHAKER LEMON SAUCE

QUANTITY	FOUR ½-PINT JARS
METHOD & SHELF LIFE	WATER BATH – 1 YEAR REFRIGERATION – 2 WEEKS

This treat from the Shakers is a basic citrus sauce that has remained unchanged through generations. The sauce is a refreshing topping for all baked puddings and cakes or even fresh fruit.

4 large eggs, preferably from free range chickens,
   at room temperature
2 cups sugar
2 cups unsalted butter
1 cup strained fresh lemon juice
1 tablespoon grated fresh lemon zest, preferably organic

Combine the eggs with the sugar, butter, lemon juice and zest in the bowl of a food processor fitted with the metal blade. Process until thoroughly combined. Scrape the mixture into the top half of a double boiler over very hot water. Cook, stirring constantly until the sauce is thick. Add drops of boiling water if you feel sauce is too thick. Remove from the heat and immediately pour into hot sterilized jars. Cap and process for 15 minutes in a boiling water bath as directed on pages 30–32.

KILLER CHOCOLATE FUDGE SAUCE

QUANTITY   FOUR ½-PINT JARS

METHOD   REFRIGERATION – 1 WEEK
&   MAY BE FROZEN – 6 MONTHS
SHELF LIFE

This is it — the ONLY one! A chocoholic's dream! The ultimate chocolate dessert sauce!

4 ounces unsweetened chocolate
6 large egg yolks, preferably from free range chickens,
    beaten, at room temperature
½ cup light brown sugar
1 tablespoon grated fresh orange zest
¼ cup heavy cream, at room temperature
½ cup unsalted butter
¼ cup liqueur of your choice, optional

Place the chocolate in the top half of double boiler over very hot water. Heat, stirring constantly until melted. Add the brown sugar, beaten egg yolks and orange zest. Cook, stirring constantly until well blended. Add the heavy cream and butter. Cook, stirring constantly until the sauce is thick. Remove from the heat. Stir in liqueur, if using. Pour into sterilized containers and refrigerate or freeze as directed on pages 32–34.

BASIC SUGAR SYRUP

QUANTITY	FOUR ½-PINT JARS
METHOD & SHELF LIFE	REFRIGERATION – 2 WEEKS MAY BE FROZEN – 6 MONTHS

After years of frustration at not having a simple syrup on hand when I was ready to poach fruit or prepare other desserts or drinks requiring it, I finally put some by. It is so easy, keeps for quite a period of time in the fridge and is a pleasure to have on hand.

4 cups sugar
4 cups cold water

Place sugar and water in a heavy saucepan over medium heat. Bring to a boil and stir constantly for 5 minutes. Remove from the heat. Pour into sterilized containers and refrigerate or freeze as directed on pages 32–34.

SPICED BLUEBERRY SYRUP

QUANTITY   FOUR ½-PINT JARS

METHOD   WATER BATH – 1 YEAR
&   REFRIGERATION – 2 WEEKS
SHELF LIFE

A wonderful syrup to use on breakfast breads such as pancakes or waffles, this also may be used as a dessert topping.

4 cups fresh blueberries, preferably organic
1 cup sugar
½ cup fresh lemon juice
¼ cup fresh orange juice
1 teaspoon ground cinnamon
¼ teaspoon ground nutmeg
2 tablespoons cornstarch dissolved in ¼ cup cold water
⅔ cup unsalted butter, at room temperature

Combine the blueberries with the sugar, lemon juice, orange juice, cinnamon and nutmeg in a heavy saucepan. Place over medium heat and bring to a boil. Lower the heat and cook for 20 minutes. Taste for sweetness and add additional sugar if necessary. Stir the cornstarch mixture into the hot berry sauce. Continue to cook, stirring, until slightly thickened. Whisk in the butter, a bit at a time. Remove from the heat. Pour into hot sterilized jars. Cap and process for 15 minutes in a boiling water bath as directed on pages 30–32.

RUM SYRUP

QUANTITY	FOUR ½-PINT JARS
METHOD & SHELF LIFE	WATER BATH – 1 YEAR REFRIGERATION – 2 WEEKS

This is a terrific multi-purpose syrup for use in soaking cakes and puddings, on waffles or in hot or cold drinks.

1 cup granulated sugar
1 cup light brown sugar
3 cups water
1 cup dark rum
1 teaspoon freshly grated lemon zest
1 cup dark raisins, optional
1 cup toasted chopped nuts, optional

Combine the granulated and brown sugars with the water in a heavy saucepan over medium heat. Bring to a boil. Lower the heat and simmer, stirring frequently, for 45 minutes. Stir in the rum and lemon zest along with the raisins and nuts, if using. Cook for 3 minutes. Remove from the heat and immediately pour into hot sterilized jars. Cap and process for 15 minutes in a boiling water bath as directed on pages 30-32.

RED HOT APPLE SYRUP

QUANTITY   FOUR ½-PINT JARS

METHOD   WATER BATH – 1 YEAR
&   REFRIGERATION – 2 WEEKS
SHELF LIFE

This spicy syrup can be used on any dessert, pancakes, waffles, French toast, crepes or as flavoring in hot or cold drinks.

5 cups fresh apple juice (see page 40), or
   fine-quality commercially canned apple juice,
   strained, preferably organic
½ cup sugar
2 cinnamon sticks, broken into pieces
1 dried red hot chili
1 large piece fresh orange peel, preferably organic
¼ cup grated fresh ginger, preferably organic

Combine the apple juice with the sugar in a heavy saucepan. Stir in the cinnamon sticks, chili, orange peel and ginger and place over medium heat. Bring to a boil. Lower the heat and simmer for 15 minutes. Remove from the heat, cover and let stand for 12 hours. Strain the cooled syrup through a fine mesh sieve, discarding the solids. Transfer the strained syrup to a heavy saucepan. Place over medium heat and bring to a boil. Lower the heat and cook for about 40 minutes or until syrup is very thick. Remove from the heat and immediately pour into hot sterilized jars. Cap and process for 15 minutes in a boiling water bath as directed on pages 30-32.

CHAPTER 10
MISCELLANY

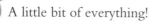

A little bit of everything!

Some recipes here are not actually preserves but are long-lasting under refrigeration.

Others are recipes for preserves to have on hand for appetizers, dips, side dishes or accompaniments.

Each has its own particular preserving or storing directions.

MISCELLANY

Flavored Vinegars • Sun-Dried Tomatoes (Pumate) • My Tapenade • Marinated Mushrooms • Aïoli • Fresh Herbs

FLAVORED VINEGARS

QUANTITY	1 QUART
METHOD & SHELF LIFE	NO PROCESSING REQUIRED
	TIGHTLY COVERED, IN A COOL DARK SPOT
	− 6 MONTHS

My pantry would not be complete without an array of fruit and herb vinegars. They make a world of difference in all recipes calling for any vinegar and are a special treat in salad dressings. I usually make one quart of each at a time. You can, of course, make as much as you want.

FRUIT VINEGAR INGREDIENTS
4 cups fine white wine vinegar (you can also use rice wine vinegar if you like the flavor)
4 cups crushed fresh berries (cranberries, blueberries, raspberries, blackberries, gooseberries, etc.) or chopped peaches or apples, preferably organic, plus a few whole berries or pieces of fruit for final processing
4 tablespoons sugar
1 strip orange peel, preferably organic

HERB VINEGAR INGREDIENTS
4 cups fine white wine vinegar or red wine vinegar
10 cloves garlic, peeled and crushed or 1 cup peeled minced shallots or 1 cup minced fresh tarragon, rosemary, sage, thyme, basil or chives
Whole pieces of garlic or shallot or 2 sprigs of the fresh herb chosen.

continued on next page

PREPARATION OF FLAVORED VINEGARS

Combine the vinegar with the fruit or herbs. Cover tightly and store in a cool, dark place, stirring daily, for 3 weeks. Strain vinegar through at least 3 layers of fine cheesecloth. Then proceed with the following directions:

For fruit vinegar: Strain into a nonreactive saucepan. Add the sugar and orange peel and bring to a boil over medium heat. Cook, stirring constantly, until sugar is dissolved. Remove from the heat. Discard orange peel and immediately pour into hot sterilized jars. Add a few fresh berries or pieces of fruit to each jar. Cover tightly and store in a cool, dark place.

For herb vinegar: Strain into a nonreactive saucepan and bring to a boil. Remove from the heat and immediately pour into hot sterilized jars. Add a few pieces of garlic or shallot or 2 sprigs of fresh herb to each jar. Cover tightly and store in a cool, dark place.

SUN-DRIED TOMATOES (PUMATE)

QUANTITY FOUR ½-PINT JARS

METHOD REFRIGERATION – 1 MONTH
&   MAY BE FROZEN – 6 MONTHS
SHELF LIFE

These can be used on pizza, in salads and sauces, as a condiment or mixed with goat cheese and with greens as a main course. If you can't purchase sun-dried tomatoes in bulk, you can dry your own. Sprinkle coarse salt on halved plum tomatoes and either place on wire racks in very hot sun for 10 days or follow the directions of a commercial home fruit dryer.

4 cups sun-dried tomatoes, preferably organic
16 basil leaves, preferably organic
8 cloves garlic, preferably organic, peeled
4 sprigs fresh rosemary, preferably organic
1 teaspoon cracked black pepper
Fine quality extra virgin olive oil

Pack 1 cup of the sun-dried tomatoes in each hot sterilized jar. Add 4 basil leaves, 2 garlic cloves, 1 sprig rosemary and ¼ teaspoon cracked black pepper to each jar. Pour in olive oil to cover. Refrigerate or freeze as directed on pages 32-34.

MY TAPENADE

QUANTITY	FOUR ½-PINT JARS
METHOD & SHELF LIFE	WATER BATH — 1 YEAR REFRIGERATION — 3 WEEKS

A wonderful sauce/condiment/relish to be used on pasta, baked potatoes, steamed vegetables or grilled fish. A perfect lunch: tossed green salad and a huge baked potato popped open and topped with tapenade and sour cream. When used with pasta, add lots of grated, fresh Parmesan cheese.

¾ cup extra virgin olive oil
3 garlic cloves, preferably organic, peeled and minced
¼ cup finely chopped onions, preferably organic
1 cup seeded and chopped green bell peppers,
  preferably organic
1 cup seeded and chopped red bell peppers,
  preferably organic
½ cup seeded and chopped yellow bell peppers,
  preferably organic
2 cups minced imported black olives
1½ cups roasted walnuts, finely chopped
⅓ cup minced fresh parsley, preferably organic
⅓ cup herb vinegar
Salt and pepper to taste
¼ cup extra virgin olive oil

Place the olive oil in heavy saucepan over medium heat and heat until just warmed. Stir in the garlic and onion and cook, stirring constantly, for 5 minutes. Stir in the green, red and yellow bell pepper then lower the heat and cook for about 10 minutes or until peppers are wilted. Add the olives, walnuts and parsley, stirring to blend. Stir in the vinegar, raise the heat to high and cook for 5 minutes or until almost all liquid has evaporated. Remove from the heat and immediately pour into hot sterilized jars. Cover each jar with 1 tablespoon of the olive oil. Cap and process for 20 minutes in a boiling water bath as directed on pages 30-32.

MARINATED MUSHROOMS

QUANTITY	½ GALLON

METHOD & SHELF LIFE	WATER BATH – 1 YEAR REFRIGERATION – 3 WEEKS

Marinated Mushrooms are favorite cocktail tidbits — easy to keep on hand and always delicious. I keep a half-gallon jar in my refrigerator at all times for use as an emergency appetizer, hors d'oeuvre or salad picker-upper. When push comes to shove, marinated mushrooms can be heated and served over pasta with lots of fresh grated cheese.

2 pounds small fresh mushrooms
8 cloves garlic, peeled
2 sprigs fresh basil
1 tablespoon grated fresh onion
1 teaspoon crushed dried red pepper flakes
2 cups fine quality olive oil
1 cup herb vinegar
½ teaspoon sugar
Dash hot pepper sauce or to taste

Combine the mushrooms with the garlic, basil, onion and red pepper flakes in a nonreactive container. Stir in the olive oil, vinegar, sugar and hot pepper sauce. Let stand for 30 minutes. Pour into a half-gallon container or a few smaller containers. Tightly cover and refrigerate for at least 24 hours before using.

AÏOLI

QUANTITY	TWO ½-PINT JARS

METHOD & SHELF LIFE	REFRIGERATED – 1 DAY MAY BE FROZEN – 3 MONTHS

Aïoli is generally used in Mediterranean cooking but it is a versatile preserve and can touch up many types of food. It is essentially a rich garlic mayonnaise. It is traditionally served with poached fish in a dish called bourride. I use it in meat or fish salads, as a main course sauce or as a vegetarian's delight covering a steamed vegetable platter.

8 large cloves garlic, peeled and chopped
2 large egg yolks, preferably from free range chickens, at room temperature
2 teaspoons fresh lemon juice or herb vinegar
¼ teaspoon salt
2 cups extra virgin olive oil

Place the garlic, egg yolks, lemon juice or vinegar and salt in a blender jar. Process at medium speed to mix thoroughly. With the motor running, slowly add the olive oil, drop by drop. Keep adding and processing until all oil is absorbed and sauce is thick. Do not overbeat, as sauce will get too thick. Scrape the sauce from the jar and pour into sterilized containers. Refrigerate or freeze as directed on page 34. If you freeze the sauce, you will have to thaw and quickly reprocess it before using.

FRESH HERBS

QUANTITY	1 CUP
METHOD	NO PROCESSING REQUIRED
&	BOTTLED – 6 MONTHS
SHELF LIFE	REFRIGERATION – 1 WEEK
	MAY BE FROZEN – 1 YEAR

These are an absolute necessity. If you grow your own, be sure to put some by for the winter months. It does make a difference in any recipe calling for herbs. There are two easy methods to preserve fresh herbs.

2 tightly-packed cups fresh herbs
¼ cup extra virgin olive oil

Bottle Method: Pack as many clean fresh herbs of one kind as you can into a ½-pint sterilized jar. Cover with extra virgin olive oil. Tightly seal and store in a cool, dark place. When ready to use, take out the amount of herb you need and use as you would fresh. You can rinse the oil off if you wish. You can also use the olive oil in salads and sauces.

Freezer Method: Place herbs and oil in a blender jar. Process until the mixture is a thick purée. Measure out tablespoons (or use physician's small disposable paper pill dispensers). Wrap in aluminum foil, seal and freeze. When frozen, put in plastic bags and label with date, amount and type of herb. This just makes it easier to use the small amounts usually required in a specific recipe.

SOURCES
Jars, Lids, Accessories and Other Supplies

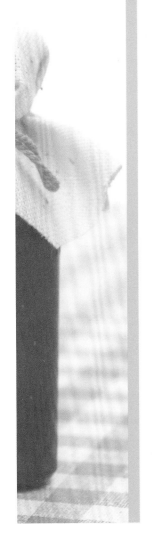

The Fresh Preserving Store
20 Constitution Boulevard South
Shelton, CT 06484
800-421-1223
www.FreshPreservingStore.com

Freund Container
877-637-3863
www.FreundContainer.com

Highland Brands
19 North 100 West
Hyrum, Utah 84319
800-285-5044
www.CanningPantry.com

Jarden Home Brands
14611 West Commerce Road
Daleville, IN 43334
888-240-3340
www.JardenHomeBrands.com

Kitchen Krafts Baking Supply
1478 Elon Drive
Waterville, Iowa 52170
888-612-1950
www.CanningSupply.com

Walmart
www.Walmart.com

Williams Sonoma
www.Williams-Sonoma.com

INDEX

190

Orange Sauterne Jelly, 49
Sealing, 30–34
  Freezing, 33–34
  Refrigeration, 32
  Water Bath, 30–32
Shaker recipes, 10–12
  Blueberry Catsup, 138
  Carrot Marmalade, 81
  Horseradish Jelly, 46
  Shaker Green Tomato Preserves, 65
  Shaker Lemon Sauce, 169
Shelf life, 36
  freezing, 33
  refrigeration, 32
  water bath canning, 31
Sichuan Pickles, 122–123
Sour Onion Pickle, 126
Soy sauce
  Teriyaki Sauce, 155
Spiced Cherries, 99
Spiced Cranberry Cassis, 98
Spiced fruits, 91, 92–99
  Ginger Pears, 94–95
  Marrons Glacés, 96–97
  Moroccan Oranges, 93
  Peaches in Port Wine, 92
  Spiced Cherries, 99
  Spiced Cranberry Cassis, 98
  Spiced Tomato Jam, 53
Spicy Beer Mustard, 133
Spirits. See Wines and spirits
Splenda® Granular No Calorie Sweetener,
  19–20, 21
Squash
  Faye's Zucchini Relish, 112–113
  Fresh Beet Relish, 115
  Pickled Baby Vegetables, 129
Steam pressure canners, 26–27
Storage, 35–See also Shelf life
Strawberries
  All-Purpose Berry Sauce, 164
  Mom's Special Strawberry Preserves, 63
  Strawberry Grand-Marnier Jam, 59
Sugar, 18
  alternatives/replacements, 18–21
  Basic Sugar Syrup, 171
  and commercial pectin, 40
Summer Relish, 120
Sun-Dried Tomatoes (Pumate), 179
Sweet sauces. See Sauces, dessert
Syrups, dessert
  Basic Sugar Syrup, 171

Red Hot Apple Syrup, 174
Rum Syrup, 173
Spiced Blueberry Syrup, 172
See also Sauces, dessert

Tapenade, 180–181
Teriyaki Sauce, 155
Tex-Mex recipes
  Basic Tex-Mex Salsa, 142–143
  Salsa Inferno, 135
  Tex-Mex Pickle, 128
Tomatoes (whole, chopped, pureed, etc.)
  Basic Tex-Mex Salsa, 142–143
  Basil Conserve, 78
  Creole Sauce, 158
  Fruit Relish, 118–119
  Gazpacho Sauce, 154
  Homemade Tomato Sauce, 160
  Hot Tomato Conserve, 75
  My Own Barbeque Sauce, 152–153
  Salsa Inferno, 135
  Shaker Green Tomato Preserves, 65
  Spiced Tomato Jam, 53
  Summer Relish, 120
  Sun-Dried Tomatoes (Pumate), 179
  Tomato Chutney, 100–101
  Vegetarian Dressing, 147
Tuna Sauce, 159
Turnips
  Nouvelle Catsup, 136–37

Vegetables
  extraction of juice, 40–41
  peeling, 40
  Pickled Baby Vegetables, 129
  preparation, 17–18
  See also specific vegetables
Vegetarian Dressing, 147
Vidalia Onion Pickle, 127
Vinegars. See Fruit Vinegars; Herb Vinegars; See
  also Pickles; Salad dressings

Walnuts
  Brandied Date Conserve, 73
  My Tapenade, 180–181
Water bath canning, 26–27, 31–32
  sealing, 30–32
What I Think Is Traditional Chutney, 106–107
White Chocolate Sauce, 163
Wines and spirits
  Apple-Brandy Butter, 85
  Basil Conserve, 78

Black Forest Preserves, 67
Blackberry Brandy Jam, 55
Bourbon Butter, 87
Brandied Date Conserve, 73
Cassis Jelly, 47
Champagne Jelly, 51
Cranberry Rum Sauce, 166
Framboise Jelly, 52
Fruit Relish, 118–119
Fruit Salad Dressing, 148
Ginger Pear Preserves, 69
Ginger Pears, 94–95
Grand-Marnier Marmalade, 83
Hot and Sour Salad Dressing, 145
Killer Chocolate Fudge Sauce, 170
Kumquat Grand-Marnier Preserves, 64
Lemon Chutney, 102
Marrons Glacés, 96–97
Mushroom Sauce, 156–157
Old Rummy, 77
Orange Sauterne Jelly, 49
Peaches in Port Wine, 92
Port Wine Jelly, 45
Praline Sauce, 168
Red Onion Marmalade, 79
Rhubarb Chutney, 104
Rum Syrup, 173
Sambuca Romana Jam, 61
Sambuca Sauce, 166
Spiced Cranberry Cassis, 98
Strawberry Grand-Marnier Jam, 59
White Chocolate Sauce, 163

Zucchini
  Faye's Zucchini Relish, 112–113
  Fresh Beet Relish, 115

_____

_____

_____

_____

_____

_____

_____

_____

_____

_____

_____

_____

_____

Notes: